Item
not
in w
bar
at y
Re
Fir
Da

BREAK A LEG!

A Dictionary of Theatrical Quotations

–

Compiled by Michèle Brown

Introduced by Gyles Brandreth

WITHDRAWN FROM STOCK
DUBLIN CITY PUBLIC LIBRARIES

Leabharlanna Poiblí Chathair Baile Átha Cliath
Dublin City Public Libraries

 Notting Hill

D0228551

Published in 2018
by Notting Hill Editions
Mirefoot, Burneside, Kendal Cumbria LA8 9AB

Cover design by Plain Creative, Kendal, Cumbria
Typeset by CB Editions
Printed and bound by Short Run Press

Copyright © 1993, 2018 by Michèle Brown

All rights reserved

The right of Michèle Brown to be identified as the compiler
of this work has been asserted in accordance with Section 77
of the Copyright, Designs and Patents Act 1998

This book is sold subject to the condition that it shall not, by way of
trade or otherwise, be lent, resold, hired out or otherwise circulated
without the publisher's prior consent in any form of binding or cover
other than that in which it is published and without a similar condition
including this condition being imposed on the subsequent purchaser

A CIP record for this book
is available from the British Library

ISBN 978–1–912559–03–9

www.nottinghilleditions.com

For Noel Davis,
who for twenty years kept me laughing with an
inexhaustible repertoire of theatrical stories

Contents

Gyles Brandreth

– Introduction –

Fifty years ago, when I was a student at Oxford University, I decided that I wanted to put on a production for the OUDS – the Oxford University Dramatic Society. My plan was to direct a traditional English pantomime, *Cinderella*, with a script by one of my literary heroes, the great Byron. No, not Lord Byron the poet, but his less-well known cousin, Henry James Byron, the playwright who created the character of Buttons for his *Cinderella* and invented Widow Twankay for his version of *Aladdin*.

To secure my OUDS production I had to audition for the OUDS President. She was an alarmingly beautiful and wonderfully gifted actress called Diana Quick, who, not long after, went on to become famous in the television series *Brideshead Revisited*. Having been given the go-ahead to direct *Cinderella*, Diana told me I needed a choreographer and pointed me in the direction of another student, Michael Coveney, who went on to become one of the most noted theatre critics of our time as well as the acclaimed biographer of Dame Maggie Smith. With Michael I set about casting the production and for our Fairy Queen we chose a young girl called Eliza Mannigham-Buller, who went on to become the head of MI5. When it came to casting the role of Cinderella we were spoilt for choice. The undergraduate actress who most caught my eye when she turned up for her audition was called Michèle Brown, who went on to become the compiler of this unique dictionary of theatrical quotations – and my wife.

Since we first met at that audition back on 6 June 1968, Michèle and I have had many theatrical adventures together. When that same year she played Viola in a student production of *Twelfth Night*, I played the Sea Captain. (Years later, I played the part again, with my daughter-in-law, the American actress Kosha Engler, as Viola.) After leaving university, and both embarking on careers in broadcasting and publishing, Michèle and I returned to Oxford in the mid-1970s when I was appointed Artistic Director of the Oxford Theatre Festival (based at the Oxford Playhouse and the New Theatre, Oxford) and we staged a series of plays with a distinguished company that included Michael Redgrave, Celia Johnson, Ian Carmichael, Sinead Cusack and Charles Dance among many others. Tom Baker (before he became Dr Who) played Oscar Wilde for us. Samuel Beckett told me I couldn't put on a musical version of *Waiting for Godot*, but could stage the first revival of his play so long as his friend Patrick Magee directed it. Michèle was on hand to help in whatever capacity was required. (She has not forgotten working through the night, painting the set for our production of *Saint Joan* when she was pregnant with our first-born who would become Benet Brandreth QC, barrister, rhetoric coach for the Royal Shakespeare Company and occasional actor: he starred in a production of *Hamlet* in London last year. I played his father. His wife Kosha Engler played his mother and Ophelia. We like to mix it up a bit, as well as keep it in the family.)

At the Oxford Theatre Festival my associate artistic

director was an actor called Noel Davis. He went on to become a leading casting director in the film industry – working notably on the films of the celebrated director John Schlesinger – but Michèle and I remember him best as the funniest man we ever knew. Nobody could tell a story quite like Noel Davis.

His real first name was Edgar, but when he left the merchant navy to become an actor he changed it to Noel in honour of the great man of twentieth-century British theatre, Sir Noël Coward. Our Noel knew all the Coward stories – and all the Laurence Olivier stories and all the Sarah Bernhardt and Mrs Patrick Campbell and Tallulah Bankhead stories too. He was a walking encyclopaedia of theatre lore.

It was Noel's stories that inspired Michèle to compile this collection of theatrical quotations. Read this book and I reckon you get the essence of theatre. It's a veritable A-to-Z of drama, from Aristotle and Aristophanes to Ziegfeld and Zeffirelli. It contains all the great lines you would expect to find in an anthology of its kind, as well as lots of surprises and lines you won't find elsewhere. It features all the greats – from Burbage to Branagh, from Oscar Wilde to Orson Welles, from Dame Ellen Terry to Dame Judi Dench – and touches, both wittily and illuminatingly, on every aspect of theatre life, front-stage and back, from the horrors of the first audition to the horrors of the opening night, from the nature of star quality to the reality of stage fright.

Over the years Michèle and I have been involved in every kind of theatrical venture. We have had hits (five West End shows) – and flops (we don't talk about those). As a performer I have appeared in pantomime, Wilde and Shakespeare. As people who have written about the theatre, we have been privileged to know some wonderful theatre folk, from the effortlessly charming Vincent Price to the trio of great dames of our day: Eileen Atkins, Judi Dench and Maggie Smith. On his ninetieth birthday, we invited the great Sir John Gielgud to join us both for lunch. The actress Glenda Jackson made up the fourth. When Sir John arrived, I told him how honoured we all felt that he should choose to celebrate his ninetieth birthday with us. 'Oh, my dears,' he replied in that beautiful fluting voice of his, 'I'm delighted. You see, all my *real* friends are dead.'

In the 1990s, I took a break from writing and the theatre to become a member of parliament. I was appearing with Bonnie Langford and Barbara Windsor in another production of *Cinderella* at the time I was selected to stand as an MP. One newspaper columnist suggested I was about to move from pantomime to farce. He wasn't that wide of the mark. After five lively years at Westminster, another election came along and the people spoke – in my case, in no uncertain terms. The curtain came down on my Whitehall farce. I had to find something else to do. I rather fancied the idea of being in a musical. I saw myself as Henry Higgins in *My Fair Lady.* And as Dorothy in *The Wizard of Oz.* And possibly even in the title role of *The Phantom of the Opera.*

Michèle suggested I get the whole lot out of my system in just one evening and so a show called *Zipp! 100 musicals in 100 Minutes, Or Your Money Back* was born. We opened on the Edinburgh Fringe in August 2002 and, having won the Most Popular Show at the Fringe Award, played to capacity before taking the production to the Duchess Theatre in London and on tour around the United Kingdom over the next two years. I have been back to Edinburgh several times since – usually in one-man shows presented in the Pleasance Courtyard by a remarkable impresario called Nigel Klarfeld of Bound & Gagged Comedy (be sure to include the word 'Comedy' if you look up the company on your computer or you may end up in court) – and most recently with a show inspired by Michèle's glorious collection of theatrical quotations. I am so happy – and so blessed – that I met her fifty years ago at that audition for Byron's *Cinderella*. You should be glad, too. If it wasn't for that chance encounter you would not be holding this very special book in your hands now.

Beginners please. House lights down. Curtain up. Turn the page. It's show time. Break a leg!

Michèle Brown

– How to Use This Book –

T he primary aim of this book is to reflect the wit and wisdom of the theatre in a wide-ranging selection of quotations which can be dipped into at random or read section by section. The titles of the sections are found in the contents list at the front of the book.

The index is biographical, giving the dates where known, and a brief description of the person concerned, then listing all references to them in the book. This index includes details of people written about (e.g. Mary Betterton) and of people quoted (e.g. George Jean Nathan). Obviously there are many people who come into both categories (e.g. Olivier). Including biographical information in the text would mean cumbersome repetition. However, understanding the wider context of the quotations enhances their value and I recommend using this index extensively.

A few conventions have been used which might possibly be unfamiliar to some readers. Ibid means that a quotation comes from the same author and source as the quotation immediately preceding it; *fl.* in the biographical index means that I do not have exact dates of birth and death of the person named but that he or she flourished around the date indicated.

ACTING

In London acting is not a capricious, freakish, or Bohemian way of life. It is an ancient and honourable profession that is accepted by the public as a normal part of the life of London.
– **Brooks Atkinson** *Broadway*, 1970

Acting is a bum's life. Quitting acting – *that* is a sign of maturity.
– **Marlon Brando**

When you act in the West End you pick up your coffee cup in exactly the same way for nine months. – **Richard Briers** *The Times*, 6 May 1992

I am acquainted with no immaterial sensuality so delightful as good acting.
– **Lord Byron** letter to Thomas Moore, 1814

All acting is a question of control, the control of the actor of himself, and through himself of the audience.
– **Noël Coward** quoted in *Great Acting* (ed. H. Burton), 1967

Acting is the shy person's revenge on the world.
– **Sinead Cusack** *Daily Mail*, 16 February 1991

I think I love and reverence all arts equally, only putting my own just above the others ... To me it seems as if when God conceived the world, that was Poetry; He formed it and that was Sculpture; He coloured it, and that was Painting; He peopled it with living beings, and that was the grand, divine, eternal Drama.
– **Charlotte Cushman**

An actor with no insecurities would be lost. – **Judi Dench** *Daily Mail*, 21 January 1992

It is easier to get an actor to be a cowboy than to get a cowboy to be an actor.
– **John Ford** attrib.

Of all the arts I think acting must be the least concrete, the most solitary. – **John Gielgud** *Early Stages*, 1938

When you finally learn how to do it you're too old for the good parts. – **Ruth Gordon** quoted in Leonard Lyons' column, 21 June 1972, when she was 76

The terrible thing about acting in the theatre is that you have to do it at night. – **Katherine Hepburn** *New York Times*, 16 January 1976

Acting isn't really a very high class way to make a living, is it? – **Katherine Hepburn**

Life's what's important. Walking, houses, family, birth and pain and joy. Acting's just waiting for the custard pie. That's all.
– **Katherine Hepburn**

Acting is painting, not photography. – **Derek Jacobi** *Sunday Times*, 24 May 1992

It is a most unholy trade.
– **Henry James**

Acting more than any other art is a demonstration of rebellion against the mundanity of everyday existence.
– **Micheal MacLiammoir**

I think the whole business of being an actor and being part of entertainment, whether it be TV shows or stage shows or movies, is noble. You learn about everything, and you're involved in something. You know what it is – it's acting. Look at the doctors and the lawyers. They think they're real people.
– **Walter Matthau**, 1979; quoted in J. Green, *A Dictionary of Contemporary Quotations*, 1982

Acting is therefore the lowest of all the arts, if it is an art at all. – **George Moore** *Mummer Worship*

The whole matter of acting is enveloped with written and oral bosh. – **George Jean Nathan** *Encyclopaedia of the Theatre*, 1940

Acting should be seen and not written about. – Ibid.

If somebody asked me to put in a sentence what acting was, I should say that acting was the art of persuasion.
– **Laurence Olivier** quoted in K. Tynan, *Curtains*, 1961

It does seem sometimes

that acting it hardly the occupation of an adult.
– **Laurence Olivier**, 1970

Acting – the ability to keep an audience from coughing.
– **Ralph Richardson**
Observer, 1947

Acting is like roller skating – once you know how to do it, it is neither stimulating nor exciting. – **George Sanders** quoted in J. Green, *A Dictionary of Contemporary Quotations*, 1982

Highly paid casual labour of the most casual sort.
– **George Bernard Shaw**

Shouting in the evening.
– **Patrick Troughton** (definition of acting)

I love acting. It is so much more real than life.
– **Oscar Wilde** *The Picture of Dorian Gray*, 1891

Acting is like painting pictures on bathroom tissues. Ten minutes later you throw them **away** and they are gone.
– **Shelley Winters** *The Saturday Evening Post*, 1962

ACTORS

The aim of an actor should not be the part, but the whole. – **Peggy Ashcroft**, 1961

A good French actor is merely a French barrister who has missed his vocation.
– **Arnold Bennett** *Journals 1896–1928*

An actor is a sculptor who carves in snow.
– **Edwin Booth**

An actor is a guy who, if you ain't talking about him, ain't listening. – **Marlon Brando** *Observer*, 1956

An actor is something less than a man, while an actress is something more than a woman. – **Richard Burton**

The better the actor the more stupid he is.
– **Truman Capote**

They are a race apart, doomed to go through life pretending to be someone else. – **R. F. Delderfield**

He speaks all his words

distinctly, half as loud again as the other. Anybody may see he is an actor. – **Henry Fielding** *Tom Jones*, 1749

Show me a great actor and I'll show you a lousy husband. – **W. C. Fields**

The more you do for an actor the worse it hates you. – **Percy Hammond** quoted in *Selected Letters of James Thurbe*r, 1981

Anyone who has been an actor any length of time does not know whether he has any true emotions or not. – **Cedric Hardwicke**

Only a true actor with a deep-seated compulsion is going to stick out the struggle that goes with being in the theatre. It's brutal, it's worse than a Marine boot-camp. – **Helen Hayes**

An actor-manager is one to whom the part is greater than the whole. – **Ronald Jeans**

Players, Sir! I look on them as no better than creatures set upon tables and joint stools to make faces and produce laughter, like dancing dogs. – **Samuel Johnson** quoted in James Boswell, *The Life of Samuel Johnson*, 1791

If there is anything I think I'd hate as a son-in-law, it's an actor, and if there's anything I think I'd hate worse than an actor as a son-in- law, it's an English actor. – **Joseph P. Kennedy** whose daughter Patricia married English actor Peter Lawford

An actor can remember his briefest notice well into senescence and long after he has forgotten his phone number and where he lives. – **Jean Kerr**

Although his traffic in entertainment can lead one to forget it, the great actor is one of nature's miracles. He brings aspects of music, poetry, literature and sculpture within the capacity of a human being and transmits them to the crowd. – **Laurence Kitchin** *Mid-Century Drama*, 1960

Actors should
called con
and inv
attr

seriously by the critics.
– **J. B. Priestley**

An actor is not quite a
human being – but then,
who is? – **George Sanders**
quoted in J. Green, *A
Dictionary of Contemp
Quotations*, 1982

A man is an actor
prince: by birth.
Sartre *Kean*, 195

A woman can
actress and
woman at
– **Clemen**

– A
Olive
New Cyn

Some of the gr
love affairs I've kn
have involved one ac
unassisted. – **Wilson M**
quoted in A. Johnson, *The
Incredible Mizners*, 1953

There
respec
stage
actr

It is a great help for a man
to be in love with himself.
For an actor it is absolutely
essential. – **Robert Morley**
quoted in his obituary, *The
Times*, 4 June 1992

Lik
Ure] w
unemploy
when appear
to full houses.
– **John Osborne** *A*
Gentleman, 1991

Actors and boarding school
misses keep scrapbooks.
– **George Jean Nathan**

Actors like Shakespeare
because they can gum on
a lot of crepe hair, bellow
almost anything that
comes into their heads,
then have their Lear tak

The autobiographies of
English and American
actresses appear to differ

5

...*rary*

s he is a
— **Jean Paul**
4

not be an
respectable
he same time
Scott

re thousands of
table women on the
and only about six
esses.
Robert Buchanan response
the above

he stock actor is a stage
lamity.
George Bernard Shaw

will never be an actor
il you have learnt to get
ugh your part though
now comes through
of; with an audience
sting of only two or

three drunks, who are not listening; while the sparrows twitter and flutter round the auditorium before settling to roost in the flies; while rats trot across the footlights carrying your pet powder-puff in their mouths. You have got to learn to act though none of the company except yourself are sober; when no one gives you your proper cue; when you have not had a square meal for a month and will probably get no salary on Saturday, when you are sent on to play a part of two or three hundred lines with one night's study and no proper rehearsal. When you can do this, and not dry up, but hold an audience, great or small, drunk or sober, stalls or gallery, or Royal Box, whether the play is good or bad, and your part actor-proof or impossible, then, and not till then, may you call yourself an actor.
— **Mrs (Fanny) Stirling** quoted in Sir Frank Benson, *My Memoirs*

When you're an actor you cease to be male or female.
— **Sybil Thorndike** quoted

in R. Findlater, *The Player Queens*, 1976

Give an actress a round, resonant voice and a long Shakespearean part, and she will have to enter smoking a pipe to avoid being acclaimed. – **Kenneth Tynan** *Curtains*, 1961

An actor is a man who can walk to the side of the stage, peer into the wings filled with dust, other actors, stagehands, old clothes and other claptrap and say, 'What a lovely view there is from this window.' – *Variety*

Very good actors never seem to talk about their art. Very bad ones never stop. – **John Whiting** *John Whiting on Theatre*, 1966

English actors act quite well but they act between the lines. – **Oscar Wilde**

You can pick out actors by the glazed look that comes into their eyes when the conversation wanders away from themselves. – **Michael Wilding**

Actors act too much. – **Nicol Williamson** *Now*, 1981

ACTORS – Individuals

EDWARD ALLEYN

And present worth in all dost so contract
As others speak, but only thou dost act.
Weare this renowne. 'Tis just, that who did give
So many Poets *life, by one should live.*
– **Ben Jonson** *To Edward Alleyn, Epigrammes*, 1616

JULIE ANDREWS

Working with Julie Andrews is like being hit over the head with a Valentine's card. – **Christopher Plummer** *Celebrity Gossip*, 1984

FRANK BENSON

When he dies, five thousand creditors will follow him to the grave. And all will shed a tear because they can't lend him a bit more. – **Harold Neilson** quoted in R. May, *The Wit of the Theatre*, 1969

MARY BETTERTON
Having, by nature, all the accomplishments required to make a perfect actress, she added to them the distinguishing characteristic of a virtuous life.
– **Charles Gildon** *The Life of Mr Thomas Betterton*, 1710

MASTER BETTY
The popularity of that baby-faced boy, who possessed not even the elements of a good actor, was a hallucination in the public mind, and a disgrace to our theatre history. – **Thomas Campbell**

I am disposed to think his talents were not fairly appreciated. It seemed as if the public resented on the grown man the extravagance of the idolatry they had lavished on the boy.
– **William Charles Macready**

EDWIN BOOTH
But as for all the rest,
There's hardly one (I may
    say none) who stands the
    Artist's test.
The Artist is a rare, rare
    breed. There were but two
    forsooth,

In all me time (the stage's
    prime!) and The Other
    One was Booth.
– **Edmund Vance Cooke** *The Other One was Booth*

ANNE BRACEGIRDLE
She seems to have been a cold, vain and interested coquette, who perfectly understood how much the influence of her charms was increased by the severity which cost her nothing, and who could venture to flirt with a succession of admirers in the just confidence that no flame which she might kindle in them would thaw her own ice. – **Thomas Macaulay** *History of England*, 1852

RICHARD BURBAGE
Which is your Burbage now?
Your best actor?
– **Ben Jonson** *Bartholomew Fair*, 1614

RICHARD BURTON
Richard Burton is so discriminating that he won't go to see a play with anybody in it but himself.
– **Elizabeth Taylor** on her then husband

CAROL CHANNING
Carol never just enters a
room. Even when she comes
out of the bathroom her
husband applauds.
– George Burns

COLLEY CIBBER
Colley Cibber, they say,
was extremely haughty as
a theatrical manager, and
very insolent to dramatists.
When he had rejected a play,
if the author desired him
to point out the particular
parts that displeased him,
he took a pinch of snuff and
answered in general terms,
'Sir, there is nothing in it to
coerce my passions.'
– George Coleman Random
Records of My Life, 1830

Cibber had the misfortune
to have Fielding as a
persistent enemy, Fielding
was severe on him for his
alterations to Shakespeare's
plays, of one of which Cibber
self-complacently said 'I
have endeavoured to make it
more like a play than I found
in Shakespeare.'
– David Patrick *Chambers
Encyclopaedia of English
Literature*, 1903

Less human genius than
God gives an ape.
– Alexander Pope *Dunciad*,
1743

KATHERINE CORNELL
The first lady of the
American theatre (as I
sometimes think of her) . . .
– Kenneth Tynan *Show*, 1961

GÉRARD DEPARDIEU
The excitement in every
Depardieu performance
is somehow rooted in this
contradiction between the
powerful physique and
the sensitivity of the spirit
within. – David Robinson
Daily Mail, 5 January 1991

More than any other actor
since Jean Gabin, Depardieu
is a national institution.
– Ibid.

CHARLES DICKENS
Ah, Mr Dickens, if it hadn't
been for them books what an
actor you would have made!
– Anonymous admirer
quoted in J. B. Van
Ameronger, *The Actor in
Dickens*, 1926

PHYLLIS DILLER
Like an old Chevrolet
starting up on a below-
freezing morning.
– **Anonymous** description
of Phyllis Diller's laugh

I treasure every moment that
I do not see her.
– **Oscar Levant**

JOHN DREW
The Beau Brummel of the
American Stage.
– **Margaret Case Harriman**

GERALD DU MAURIER
When one knew him, one
knew that the stage meant
nothing to him but a means
of getting money; he never
pretended otherwise.
– **A. A. Milne** *It's Too Late
Now* (autobiography), 1939

ROBERT ELLISTON
His feelings follow each
other like the buckets on a
water-wheel, full one instant
and empty the next.
– **Leigh Hunt**

EDITH EVANS
As earthy as a potato, as
slow as a cart-horse, and as
cunning as a badger.

– **W. A. Darlington**
reviewing her Nurse in
Romeo and Juliet, 1935

To me, Edith looks like
something that would eat its
young.
– **Dorothy Parker**

BARRY FITZGERALD
He could steal a scene from a
dog. – **John Ford**

MINNIE MADDERN FISKE
Somewords she runstogether,
Some others are distinctly
    stated.
Somecometoofast and
S o m e   t o o   s l o w
And some are sy$^{n}_{c}{}^{o}_{p}{}^{a}$ted
And yet no voice – I am
    sincere –
Exists that I prefer to hear.
– **Franklin P. Adams** *c.*1918;
quoted in Brooks Atkinson,
Broadway, 1970

FRÉDÉRICK
There was always something
offensive to good taste in
Frederick's acting – a note
of vulgarity, partly owing
to his daring animal spirits
but mainly owing, I suspect,
to an innate vulgarity of
nature. – **G. H. Lewes**

On Actors and the Art of Acting, 1875

ALEC GUINNESS
The number of arrests following the circulation of his description would break all records.
– **Kenneth Tynan**

NELL GWYNNE
. . . so great performance of a comical part was never, I believe, in the world before as Nell hath done this, both as mad girle, and then, most and best of all, when she comes in like a young gallant; and hath the motions and carriage of a spark, the most that ever I saw any man have. It makes me, I confess, admire her.
– **Samuel Pepys** on Nell Gwynne's performance as Florimel in Dryden's *Mayden Queene* in *Diary*, 2 March 1667

CEDRIC HARDWICKE
You are my fifth favourite actor, the first four being the Marx Brothers.
– **George Bernard Shaw**

RICHARD HARRIS
He's something of a f—-up, no question. – **Charlton Heston** *Celebrity Gossip*, 1984

KATHERINE HEPBURN
Katherine of Arrogance.
– **Anon.**

She has a cheekbone like a death's head allied to a manner as sinister and aggressive as crossbones.
– **James Agate**

She has a face that belongs to the sea and the wind, with large rocking-horse nostrils and teeth that you just know bite an apple a day.
– **Cecil Beaton**

HEDDA HOPPER
Hedda Hopper was a dud actress who swapped the stage for journalism.
– **Simone Signoret**

CELIA JOHNSON
She was the middle-class doctor's daughter who became an actress because she thought it would be 'rather wicked'. – **Kate Fleming** (daughter) *The Mail on Sunday*, 13 October 1991

JOHN KEMBLE

Frogs in a marsh, flies in a bottle, wind in a crevice, a preacher in a field, the drone of the bagpipe, all yielded to the inimitable soporific monotony of Mr Kemble.
– **George Coleman Random** *Records of My Life*, 1830

Kemble turned his head so slowly that people might have imagined he had a stiff neck, while his words followed so slowly that he might have been reckoning how many words he had got by heart. – **Leigh Hunt** *Critical Essays on Performers in the London Theatre*, 1807

He never pulls out his handkerchief without a design upon the audience.
– Ibid.

DEBORAH KERR

Miss Kerr is a good actress. She is also unreasonably chaste. – **Laurence Olivier**

LILLIE LANGTRY

I would rather have discovered Mrs Langtry than have discovered America.
– **Oscar Wilde** October 1882

GERTRUDE LAWRENCE

Most actresses when they write a book about their youth recall the crunch of carriage wheels in the drive. Gertie recalled eating kippers in the gutter, which, of course, was completely untrue. – **Noël Coward** *Present Indicative*, 1937

She had this shimmering kind of sexual, sensuous elegance, like a perfume wafting over you.
– **Daniel Massey** BBC TV, 1 March 1992

BEA LILLIE

She could make me laugh reading from the telephone book. – **Ashton Stevens** review 1926; quoted in Bea Lillie, *Every Other Inch a Lady*, 1972

WALTER MATTHAU

He could play anything from Rhett Butler to Scarlett O'Hara. – **Billy Wilder** *Time*, 24 May 1971

DAVID NIVEN

I always knew that if all else failed I could be an actor – and all else failed. – **David Niven**

IVOR NOVELLO
The two most beautiful things in the world are Ivor's profile and my mind.
– **Noël Coward**

PETER O'TOOLE
The very stereotype of the ham. – **Omar Sharif** quoted in *Celebrity Gossip*, 1984

ANTHONY QUAYLE
You'll never be out of work for long, and I'll tell you why. Because you are a bloody good actor: – and you haven't enough personality to worry a leading man.
– **Laurence Olivier** quoted in A. Quayle, *A Time to Speak*, 1990

RACHEL
The strife, the mixture in her soul, are ours; Her genius and her glory are her own. – **Matthew Arnold** quoted in M. Billington, *The Guinness Book of Theatre Facts and Feats*, 1982

Her range, like *Kean's*, was very limited, but her expression was perfect within that range.
– **G. H. Lewes**

On Actors and the Art of Acting, 1875

BASIL RATHBONE
I don't know what his name is but he has a face like two profiles stuck together.
– **Mrs Patrick Campbell**

VANESSA REDGRAVE
She's a marvellous actress and she never stops coming out with new plays, and she manages to find time for all that political rubbish as well.
– **John Gielgud** *Daily Mail*, 16 August 1991

MARGARET RUTHERFORD
A British comedienne whose appearance suggests an overstuffed electric chair.
– *Time* 1962; review of *Murder She Says*

ATHENE SEYLER
An irritable hippopotamus.
– **Anonymous critic** quoted in her obituary, *The Times*, 13 September 1990

THOMAS SHERIDAN
Sherry is dull, naturally dull; but it must have taken him a great deal of pains to become what we now see him. Such

an excess of stupidity, sir, is not nature.
– **Samuel Johnson**, 28 July 1763; quoted in J. Boswell, *Life of Samuel Johnson*, 1791

ELIZABETH TAYLOR
She has an incipient double chin, her legs are too short and she has a slight pot belly.
– **Richard Burton** Miss Taylor's husband at the time, 1967

She's not acting at all. She doesn't know how.
– **Walter Kerr**

MARIE TEMPEST
Every new appearance of Miss Marie Tempest is a fresh delight. True, she is always presenting the same thing – herself. But hers is a very various self, and she can always find you some unanticipated *nuance*, some very latest fashion of herself, like the very latest fashion of her gowns. – *The Times*, 6 September 1891

SYBIL THORNDIKE
She could act with a tailor's dummy and bring it to life.
– **Ralph Richardson**

PETER USTINOV
I was irrevocably betrothed to laughter, the sound of which has always seemed to me the most civilized music in the universe. – **Peter Ustinov** *Dear Me*, 1977

ORSON WELLES
He is too big for the boots of any part. – **Kenneth Tynan** reviewing Welles as Captain Ahab in the 1955 London production of *Moby Dick*

I started at the top and worked down.
– **Orson Welles**

MAE WEST
A plumber's idea of Cleopatra. – **W. C. Fields**

Because my plays have dealt with sex and the dregs of humanity, some persons see fit to assume that I write vividly about such subjects because I know them by experience . . . People who know me will bear me out that there is no star who is less of an exhibitionist, or who shows herself less in public places than myself. I am, in fact, retiring by nature in my private life to the point of shyness . . . I do not drink. I do not smoke. I have my books, my writings, my friends – that is my private life. – **On herself**

I'm just a campfire girl.
– **On herself**

DONALD WOLFIT

At the end of every barnstorming performance Wolfit would stagger back on stage clinging to the curtains as though drained to the dregs and on his knees. The audience would clap in tumultuous applause as he gazed down at them with tears in his eyes. When the final curtain went down Wolfit would say: 'Coughing bastards', and leg it at full speed to his dressing room and a drink.
– **Alan Ayckbourn** *Daily Mail*, 1 October 1991

Olivier is a *tour de force* and Wolfit is forced to tour.
– **Hermione Gingold** after Olivier's amazing success as Richard III, 1944; quoted in R. Harwood, *Donald Wolfit*, 1971

MONTY WOOLLEY

Mr Woolley reduced the nurse in *The Man Who Came to Dinner* to the potency of a pound of wet Kleenex. It was probably the best thing that happened to the art of the insult since the Medicis stopped talking in the 16th Century.
– **Richard Severo** recollection of Monty Woolley in the role based on writer Alexander Woollcott, obituary *New York Herald-Tribune*, 7 May 1963

See also: Peggy Ashcroft, Tallulah Bankhead, The Barrymores, Sarah Bernhardt, Mrs Patrick Campbell, Critical Abuse – Actors; Garrick, John Gielgud, Irving, Kean, Vivien Leigh, Oscar Levant, The Lunts, Laurence Olivier, Ralph Richardson, Shakespeare's Plays, Sarah Siddons, Ellen Terry, H. B. Tree.

ADAPTATIONS

Dramatisations as a rule prove more like sieves than

containers for the virtues of a book. – **John Mason Brown**

I don't want to see the uncut version of ANYTHING. – **Jean Kerr**

ADVICE

Remember, Ernest my boy, steak and stout for tragedy. – **Henry Ainley** to Ernest Milton; quoted in D. Blakelock, *Acting My Way*

Get on, say the wordies loud and clear, and get off. – **Pamela Brown**

Forget about the motivation. Speak the lines clearly and don't trip over the furniture. – **Noël Coward**

You've got to keep surprising them. Always come out of another hole. – **Noël Coward** to David Lean; recounted by David Lean at the 1989 Academy Awards Dinner

Don't put your daughter on the stage, Mrs Worthington,

Don't put your daughter on the stage, The profession is overcrowded And the struggle's pretty tough And admitting the fact She's burning to act, That isn't quite enough. – **Noël Coward** 'Mrs Worthington' (song), *The Lyrics of Noël Coward*, 1965

My entire success is based on one rule: never take advice from anybody. – **W. C. Fields** to Paul Muni, quoted in Jerome Lawrence, *Actor: The Life and Times of Paul Muni*, 1974

Well, of course, if you can't love him you'll never be any good in him, will you? – **Tyrone Guthrie** to Laurence Olivier on his Sergius Saranoff in *Arms and the Man*, 1944. Olivier later called this 'the richest pearl of advice in my life'. Quoted in A. Holden, *Olivier*, 1988.

My boy listen to me. In the next twenty or thirty years you may be called upon to perform some

eight thousand times, and as you may possibly not feel inspired each time you perform you may, during the course of a very stren-u-ous role, not feel inspired more than – er – let us say – um – ten minutes per act. I think therefore, you will do well to remember that by taking great pains you can, shall we say – um – design a part, a role, so carefully that, inspired or not, you'll be demmed interesting. The less 'feeling' the better. See what I mean, my boy.
– **Henry Irving** quoted in Edward Gordon Craig, *Henry Irving*, 1930

Watch, watch always, and if you see nothing worth copying, you will see something to avoid.
– **Henry Irving** to Constance Benson quoted in Constance Benson, *Mainly Players*, 1926

I once got a letter from Richard Burton . . . He had seen me in a student *Hamlet*, and he wrote that I suffered from the same thing he did: a voice too melodious, easy to listen to and liable to send people to sleep. He advised me to roughen it up a bit.
– **Derek Jacobi** *Sunday Times*, 24 May 1992

Anyone who works is a fool. I don't work – I merely inflict myself on the public.
– **Robert Morley**

My dear boy, why don't you try acting – it's so much easier. – **Laurence Olivier** to Dustin Hoffman. (For the film *Marathon Man* Dustin Hoffman had stayed awake for several nights in order to be convincing as a man who had had no sleep.)

If you're going on the stage, read Dickens, and you'll never lack for a characterisation. – **Laurence Olivier** quoted in *Great Acting* (ed. H. Burton), 1967

Just remember there's many an actor sleeping on the embankment tonight, with no soles to his shoes, for lack of an upward inflection.
– **Douglas Quayle** to his son John Quayle when he decided on an acting career; recalled by Donald Sinden

The most important advice I ever had came from a Hungarian teacher who told me every actress has to be aware of outside influences, or poodles. If you are to be a good actress you must let your poodles off the leash and stop thinking about them.

– **Vanessa Redgrave** *Evening Standard*, 13 November 1991

. . . the greatest difficulty is to keep sober enough in the one hour twenty five minutes wait you have before the end to take your curtain call without falling into an orchestra pit. This takes years of skill and cannot be overestimated, as much of the effect of the poetic 'Mab' speech may be lost by such an incident. . . .

– **Ralph Richardson** to Laurence Olivier; letter on his experience playing Mercutio in *Romeo and Juliet*; quoted in F. Barker, Laurence Olivier, 1984

Speak the speech, I pray you, as I pronounced it to you, trippingly on the tongue; but if you mouth it, as many of your players do, I had as lief the town-crier spoke my lines. Nor do not saw the air too much with your hand, but use all gently; for in the very torrent, tempest, and as I may say, the whirlwind of your passion, you must acquire and beget a temperance that may give it smoothness.

– **William Shakespeare** *Hamlet*, Act III, Scene 2

Suit the action to the word, the word to the action, with this special observance, that you o'erstep not the modesty of nature. – Ibid.

There are no small parts, only small actors.

– **Constantin Stanislavski**; often attributed to other actors, e.g. **Ginger Rogers**

The three great I's are Industry, Intelligence and Imagination: and the greatest of these is Imagination.

– **Ellen Terry** to Gwen Ffrangcon-Davies; recalled by her in *The Times*, 26 January 1991

Keep your bowels and your vowels open.
– **Herbert Beerbohm Tree**

I always pass on good advice. It is the only thing to do with it. – **Oscar Wilde** *An Ideal Husband*, 1899

AMATEURS

A professional is a man who can do his job when he doesn't feel like it; an amateur is one who can't do it when he does feel like it.
– **James Agate** (the difference between professional and amateur actors)

The artistic temperament is a disease that attracts amateurs.
– **G. K. Chesterton** *Heretics*

Those brave individuals who always step in where audiences fear to tread.
– **Seymour Hicks** *Chestnuts Reroasted*

AMBITION

I am only interested in two kinds of people; those who can entertain me and those who can advance my career.
– **Ingrid Bergman**

I think I've left it a bit late. I might play the nurse in *Romeo and Juliet*.
– **Noël Coward** when asked if he still had any ambition to play a Shakespearean role

To be Bernard Shaw is honour enough.
– **George Bernard Shaw** when offered a knighthood

I've been offered tides, but I think they get one into disreputable company.
– **George Bernard Shaw** on his 90th birthday, 1946

You know, you get frightfully cocky, but if you haven't got that in the theatre, if you don't feel, 'I've got something to say that nobody else on this earth knows how to say,' I don't think you're any good.
– **Sybil Thorndike** quoted in R. Findlater, *The Player Queens*, 1976

ARTISTIC INTEGRITY

My memory is full of beauty – Hamlet's soliloquies, the Queen Mab speech, King Magnus's monologue from *The Apple Cart*. Do you expect me to clutter up all that with this horse-shit?
– **John Barrymore** when refusing to learn the lines for his movie roles

PEGGY ASHCROFT

She was a great actress because she was a great woman; so when we are responding to Ashcroft the actress we are also responding to a unique woman. – **Michael Billington** TV obituary, 17 June 1991

What a huge hole she's left. She was more than an actress. She rallied the troops.
– **Judi Dench** *Sunday Times*, 15 December 1991

In her steady progress towards the heights of her art Peggy Ashcroft learned to subsume her youthfulness, charm, delicacy and Englishness in the truths of the characters that she not only played but lived. – **Richard Findlater** *The Player Queens*, 1976

When Peggy came on in the Senate scene it was as if all the lights in the theatre had suddenly gone up.
– **John Gielgud** on her Desdemona in *Othello*, 1930

It was like being butted in the stomach by a young calf.
– **John Gielgud** on acting with Peggy Ashcroft in *Romeo and Juliet*, 1932; TV obituary, 17 June 1991

More than any other actress on the stage she has the moral alertness which separates the tragic from the merely melodramatic or pathetic.
– **Penelope Gilliatt** review of *The Duchess of Malfi*, 1960

When I told her that she was a potato in Leicester – that the theatre bar there had a 'Spud Ashcroft' stuffed with prawns, she took both hands off the wheel and waved them about with pleasure and amazement. We nearly hit a lorry. – **Peter Hall** *Diaries*, 21 April 1974

She cared more about the play than the part, and more about the company than being a star. She fought tirelessly for serious theatre, and was always there when a new start was made.
– **Peter Hall** *Sunday Times*, 16 June 1991

AUDIENCES

Long experience has taught me that in England nobody goes to the theatre unless he or she has bronchitis.
– **James Agate** *Ego* 8, 1947

The best audience is intelligent, well-educated, and a little drunk.
– **Alben W. Berkley**

Audiences, no, the plural is impossible. Whether it is in Butte, Montana or Broadway it's an audience. The same great hulking monster with

four thousand eyes and forty thousand teeth.
– **John Barrymore** quoted in R. May, *The Wit of the Theatre*, 1969

How many idiots go to make up a public?
– **Pierre Beaumarchais** quoted in A. Houssaye, *Behind the Scene of the Comédie Française*

In the theatre the audience wants to be surprised – but by things they expect.
– **Tristan Bernard** *Contes, Répliques et Bons Mots*

The Marquess and Marchioness of Empty are in front again.
– **Mrs Patrick Campbell** usual remark when faced with a thin house

Those who have free seats for the play hiss first.
– **Chinese proverb**

Just say the lines as written. There will be some in the audience who won't understand yet will deeply admire them.
– **Corneille**, admitting to an

actor that he did not always know the meaning of what he had written; T. Revesz, *Bolcsek Mosolya*, 1960, quoted in P. Hay, *Theatrical Anecdotes*, 1987

The great public refuse to be impressed by the Brechts and the Anouilhs and all the rest of the defeatists, and continue unregenerately to enjoy being amused in the theatre. I expect that the public will win in the long run; it usually does.
– **Noël Coward** *The Noël Coward Diaries*, February 1957 (pub. 1982)

The audience was tremendously fashionable, and for the first part of the play [*Bitter Sweet*], almost as responsive as so many cornflour blancmanges.
– **Noël Coward**

Now the common haunters [of the theatre] are for the most part, the lewdest persons in the land, apt for pilfery, peijury, forgery, or any rogueries; the very scum, rascality, and baggage of the people, thieves, cut-purses, shifters – briefly an unclean generation, and spawn of vipers . . . For a play is like a sincke in a Towne, whereunto all the filth doth runne: or a boyle in the body, that draweth all the ill humours to it.
– **Henry Crosse** 1603

By sitting on the stage, if you be a Knight, you may happily get yourself a Mistresse: if a mere Fleet Street Gentleman, a wife.
– **Thomas Dekker** *The Gull's Handbook*, 1609

No one can fully appreciate the fatuity of human nature until he has spent some time in a box office.
– **St. John Ervine**

It is extraordinary how an audience as a whole is sharper than any single member of it.
– **Peter Hall** *Diaries*, 19 October 1977

The author seeks to keep from
  me
The murderer's identity
And you are not a friend of
  his

*If you keep shouting who it
   is . . .*
– **A. P. Herbert** poem 'To
the Lady Behind Me at the
Theatre'

I always enjoy appearing
before a British audience.
Even if they don't feel like
laughing they nod their
heads to show they've
understood. – **Bob Hope**

I would produce *Noah's
Ark* in modem dress. The
curtain will not rise until
the last straggler is in his
seat. Then Noah will appear
and announce, 'Now it's
going to rain for forty days.'
At this point the ceiling in
the theatre will open and
drench the entire audience.
If they try to escape I will be
standing by the exit with a
hose to catch them.
– **George S. Kaufman**
planning his revenge on
habitual latecomers

The critic says: this is an
extremely bad play – why is
that? The audience says: this
is an extremely bad play –
why was I born? – **Jean Kerr**

It is well understood by
every dramatist that a
late-dining audience needs
several minutes of dialogue
before it recovers from its
bewilderment at finding
itself in a theatre.
– **A. A. Milne**

Besides this perpetual
pelting (with rotten
oranges) from the gallery,
which renders an English
playhouse so uncomfortable,
there is no end to their
calling out and knocking
with their sticks 'til the
curtain is drawn up.
– **Dr Moritz** on 18th-century
English audiences *The Era
Almanack* 1872

Adulterers, Whore-
masters, Panders, Whores
and such like effeminate,
idle, unchaste, lascivious,
graceless persons were the
most assiduous Play-hunters
in their time.
– **Ovid** *Ars Amatoria* 1 BC

*There still remains to mortify
   a wit,
The many-headed monster of
   the pit.*
– **Horace** *Epistle I*, Book II

Aunt Edna – a nice, respectable, middle-class, middle-aged maiden lady with time on her hands and money to help her pass it.
– **Terence Rattigan** on a typical member of the London audience

I don't think actors really love their audience; they are more in the nature of a lion-tamer. – **Ralph Richardson** quoted in *Great Acting* (ed. H. Burton), 1967

It is clear to me that we shall not become a play-going people until we discard our fixed idea that it is the business of the people to come to the theatre and substitute for it the idea that it is the business of the theatre to come to the people.
– **George Bernard Shaw**

I regret to say that the patrons of the gallery at the Princess's, being admitted at half the usual West End price, devote the saving to the purchase of sausages to throw at the critics. I appeal to the gentleman or lady who successfully aimed one at me to throw a cabbage next time, as I am a vegetarian, and sausages are wasted on me.
– **George Bernard Shaw**

*In other things the knowing
    artist may
Judge better than the people;
    but a play,
(Made for delight, and for no
    other use)
If you approve it not, has no
    excuse.*
– **Edmund Waller** prologue to *The Maid's Tragedy*

I want to thank you for your very generous applause – and your very heavy breathing. – **Mae West**

The play was a great success, but the audience was a total failure.
– **Oscar Wilde** after the unsuccessful first night of *Lady Windermere's Fan*, 1892

The audience strummed their catarrhs. – **Alexander Woollcott**

AUDIENCE ASIDES

Thank goodness I have
at last found a place
where I can see and hear
comfortably.
– **Anonymous woman** who
had just fallen from the
overcrowded gallery into the
pit. *The Era Almanack*,1872;
quoted in G. Snell, *The Book
of Theatre Quotes*, 1982

How different, how very
different, from the home-life
of our own dear Queen!
– **Victorian theatre-goer**
after watching Sarah
Bernhardt's frenzied
performance as the Queen
of Egypt in Shakespeare's
Antony and Cleopatra

How different, how very
different, from the home life
of our own dear queens.
– **Member of the audience**
at Wyndham's Theatre
after a performance of the
American homosexual
comedy *The Boys in the Band*

Rather an unpleasant family
those Lears. – **Comment**
during a performance of
King Lear; quoted in W.

Pett Ridge, *A Story Teller*

And the funny thing is
(pause) – exactly the same
thing happened to Dorothy.
– **Comment** after a
performance of *Vivat Vivat
Regina* 1970 (in which Mary
Queen of Scots is beheaded);
recalled by Eileen Atkins

Well Mildred, that was the
worst play I've seen since
King Lear. – Overheard
by director **John Fernald**
after a Saturday matinee
of his production of *The
Cherry Orchard*, Liverpool
Playhouse, 1948; recalled by
Noel Davis

Look, here comes old Ginger
again! – **Reaction** to the
carrot-red wig sported by
Olivier for Hotspur in *Henry
IV* Part I 1945. Overheard by
John Mills and quoted in A.
Holden, *Olivier*, 1988

AUDITIONS

The nicest words I know in
the theatre are 'That's all,
sir,' which signify the end of
a mass audition. It means we

shan't hear *Phil The Fluter's Ball* again that morning.
– **Noël Coward**

Don't worry my dear, I know how frightening this is: I had to audition for Ellen Terry.
– **Gwen Ffrangcon-Davies** while conducting a master class on *Romeo and Juliet* in 1988 at the age of 97; quoted in her obituary in *The Times*, 28 January 1992

Aspiring player auditioning for James Quin at Drury Lane: To be or not to be, that is the question.
James Quin: No question, sir, 'pon my honour – not to be, most certainly.

Callow young director to veteran actress Athene Seyler: And what have you done, Miss Seyler?
Athene Seyler: Do you mean this morning?

AVANT-GARDE

Avant-garde is French for off-Broadway garbage.
– Line from the Dick Van Dyke television show;

quoted in D. Richards, *The Curtain Rises*, 1966

The dead theatre is always with us, and what blazes from the stage today becomes an orthodoxy tomorrow. – **Peter Brook** quoted by Howard Brenton in *The Times*, 13 April 1992

I have never written for the intelligentsia. Sixteen curtain-calls and close on Saturday. – **Noël Coward**

The Theatre of the Absurd strives to express its sense of the senselessness of the human condition and the inadequacy of the rational approach by the open abandonment of rational devices and discursive thought. – **Martin Esslin** *The Theatre of the Absurd*, 1962

The one thing constant in a changing world is the avant-garde. – **Louis Jouvet**

BAD HABITS

Cocaine isn't habit forming.

I should know – I've been using it for years.
– **Tallulah Bankhead**

He was suffering from the effects of nervousness and its antidotes.
– **Constance Benson** about George Weir after he had forgotten all his lines

Ladies and gentlemen, you see that I am not in good condition to play tonight. But if you will only wait five minutes, while I go behind the scenes to cool my head in a pail of water, I'll come out and show you the damnedest King Henry you ever saw in your life.
– **Junius Brutus Booth** after being hissed for his inebriated performance in *Henry IV* at the Old Bowery Theatre, New York

Where's the stage – and what's the play?
– **Junius Brutus Booth** arriving at the theatre to play in *King Lear*

When I played drunks I had to remain sober because I didn't know how to play them when I was drunk.
– **Richard Burton**

My idea of a good afternoon's exercise is 50 Turkish cigarettes and a box of marrons glacés.
– **Noël Coward** quoted by Daniel Massey, TV interview, March 1992

Sobriety's a real turn-on for me. You can see what you're doing. – **Peter O'Toole**

It is better to drink a little too much than much too little. – **Herbert Beerbohm Tree** attrib.

Cocaine is God's way of saying you're making too much money.
– **Robin Williams**

TALLULAH BANKHEAD

More of an act than an actress. – **Anon**.

A parrot around Tallulah must feel as frustrated as a kleptomaniac in a piano store.– **Fred Allen** attrib.

I'm as pure as driven slush.
– **Tallulah Bankhead**
Observer, 24 February 1957

Don't look now, Tallulah,
but your show's slipping.
– **Heywood Broun** review of
The Exciters

Watching Tallulah on
stage is like watching
someone skating on thin
ice – everyone wants to be
there when it breaks. – **Mrs
Patrick Campbell** quoted in
Bankhead's obituary, *The
Times*, 13 December 1968

My messages to Congress
Are a lot of boola-boola.
I'm not so fond of Bankhead,
But I'd love to meet Tallulah.
– **George M. Cohen**
(Tallulah's father was
Speaker of the House of
Representatives.)

With Tallulah a leading man
has an exhausting time
– **Donald Cook** attrib. *c.*1950

A day away from Tallulah is
like a month in the country.
– **Howard Dietz** attrib.,
Show Business Illlustrated,
17 October 1961

She learned how little it
takes to make people bleed,
and sometimes she could
not resist demonstrating her
skill at this unpleasing game.
– **Brendan Gill** *New Yorker*
17 October 1972

Tallulah was crowding
seventeen when she arrived
from Alabama, stage-struck,
sultry-voiced, and brimming
with a rose-leaf beauty
which she determinedly hid
under the then fashionable
mask of white powder, blue
eye-shadow and beef-
coloured lipstick. She fondly
believed that this made
her look more like Ethel
Barrymore, who was her
idol.
– **Margaret Case Harriman**
The Vicious Circle, 1951

Tallulah was sitting in a
group of people giving
the monologue she always
thought was conversation.
– **Lillian Hellman**

I've just spent an hour
talking to Tallulah
Bankhead for a few minutes.
– **Fred Keating**

I've staged shows that called for the management of a herd of buffalo, and I've shot actors out of cannons for fifty feet into the arms of an adagio dancer, but both of them were easier than saying 'Good morning' to Miss Bankhead. – **Billy Rose**

I suppose you could say Tallulah was a tramp, in the elegant sense.
– **Tennessee Williams**

[She was] talking so ceaselessly that you had to make a reservation five minutes ahead to get a word in. – **Earl Wilson**

J. M. BARRIE

What I think I liked best was tearing up the programme and dropping the bits on people's heads.
– **Anonymous child** who had been taken to see *Peter Pan* by J. M. Barrie

The ideal audience for this would be a house composed entirely of married couples who had never had any children, or parents who had lost them all.
– **James Agate** on *Peter Pan* in *Ego 3*, 1937

In the days when Bernard Shaw was a critic he began an article on a play of mine with the words: 'This is worse than Shakespeare.' I admit that this rankled.
– **J. M. Barrie** quoted in R. May, *The Wit of the Theatre*, 1969

Dinner guest: Not all your plays are successes I suppose, Sir James? **J. M. Barrie:** No, some Peter out and some Pan out.

A little child whom the Gods have whispered to.
– **Mrs Patrick Campbell** letter to George Bernard Shaw, January 1913

The cheerful clatter of Sir James Barrie's cans as he went round with the milk of human kindness.
– **Philip Guedalla** 'Some Critics', *Supers and Supermen*, 1920

29

Oh, for an hour of Herod.
– **Anthony Hope** at the
opening of *Peter Pan*, 1904

Sugar without the diabetes.
– **George Jean Nathan**

THE BARRYMORES

ETHEL

Miss Barrymore . . . did what
came naturally to her; took
the stage, filled it, and left
the rest of us to stage rear.
– **Edward G. Robinson** *All
My Yesterdays*

JOHN

John Barrymore was Icarus,
who flew so close to the sun
that the wax on his wings
melted and he plunged back
to earth – from the peak
of classical acting to the
banalities of show business.
– **Brooks Atkinson**
Broadway, 1970

Barrymore cut through the
darkness of the theatre like a
sharp, glittering pen-knife.
– **Brooks Atkinson** quoted
in Alma Power-Waters, *John
Barrymore*

My only regret in the theatre
is that I could never sit out
front and watch me.
– **John Barrymore**

In some paradoxical fashion,
the very manner in which
Barrymore seemed almost
to revel in his disintegration
convinced people who had
never seen him in *Hamlet*
and *The Jest* that he must
have been among the giants.
– **Gene Fowler** *Good Night
Sweet Prince*, 1942

I always said that I'd like
Barrymore's acting till the
cows came home. Well,
ladies and gentlemen, last
night the cows came home.
– **George Jean Nathan** on
Barrymore's performance in
My Dear Children, 1940

Conspicuously unclean and
smelled highly on many
occasions. – **David Niven**

When I saw what they
looked like in daylight my
ulcer was cured.
– **Jack Warner** on the
notorious Hollywood 'hell-
raisers' John Barrymore and
Errol Flynn

LIONEL

Of the three Barrymores, Lionel was the one most at odds with the theatre. His attitude towards it amounted to a psychosis. He needed it; he had plenty of talent for it. But he was not a public person. He was happier – though less successful – in private occupations like painting, sculpting, etching, composing music and writing. – **Brooks Atkinson** *Broadway*, 1970

Lionel uses words only to flog them. He makes them suffer. – **John Barrymore** on his brother

MAURICE

This founder of the house of Barrymore was English-born Herbert Blyth – pre-eminently a man's man, and beyond question a woman's man, of a wit so telling and yet so good hearted that even the objects of his keen satire joined in laughter at their own expense. On the stage he was always a picture – in private an Apollo in a slop suit. Amateur champion middle-weight boxer,

narrator of a thousand stories, quick in resentment of an insult, generous to a foe, burner of candles at both ends, Bedouin of Broadway, this was the Barrymore that I knew. – **Otis Skinner** *Footlights and Spotlights*, 1924

BEAUMONT AND FLETCHER

They lived together on the Banke side, not far from the Playhouse, both batchelors; lay together; had one Wench in the house between them, which they did so admire; the same cloathes and cloake &c. betweene them.
– **John Aubrey**

For ten pounds Beaumont and Fletcher will give you any one of a dozen plays – each indistinguishable from the other. – **Caryl Brahms** *No Bed for Bacon*

I have never been able to distinguish the presence of Fletcher during the life of Beaumont, nor the absence of Beaumont during the survival of Fletcher.

– **Samuel Taylor Coleridge** *Notes for Lecture on Beaumont and Fletcher*

Dear Edith, you spoil the rhythm by putting in a 'very'. The line is 'On a clear morning you can see Marlow'. On a very clear day you can also see both Beaumont and Fletcher. – **Noël Coward** to Edith Evans in rehearsal

Though he [Fletcher] treated love in perfection, yet Honour, Ambition, Revenge, and generally all the stronger Passions he either touch'd not or not masterly. To conclude all; he was a limb of Shakespeare. – **John Dryden** Preface to *Troilus and Cressida*

The blossoms of Beaumont's imagination draw no sustenance from the soil, but are cut and slightly withered flowers stuck into sand. – **T. S. Eliot**

How I doe love thee Beaumont, and thy Muse. – **Ben Jonson** 'To Francis Beaumont' *Epigrammes*, 1616

The pair wrote a great deal that was pretty disgraceful, but at least they had been educated out of the possibility of writing Titus Andronicus. – **George Bernard Shaw** *Saturday Review*, 19 February 1898

BEGINNINGS

There was some gay, provocative dialogue, only one line of which I can recall: 'Crumbs! How exciting.' – **Noël Coward** (on his stage debut) *Present Indicative*, 1937

The boy who took the part of Kate made a fine, bold, blackeyed hussy badly in need of taming. I cannot remember seeing any actress in the part who looked it better. – **W. A. Darlington** 1922 on Laurence Olivier, aged fourteen, in *The Taming of the Shrew*

I got all the schooling any actress needs. That is, I learned to write enough to sign contracts. – **Hermione Gingold** *How to*

Grow Old Disgracefully, 1988

A young gentleman by name Mr Gravel has commenced an Actor on Account of his debts, for He is accounted an Extravagant young Fellow ... The people in general here rather pity than condemn him: this is the consequence of loose morals and may serve him as a lesson to others.
– Contemporary account of American actor **Samuel Greville**'s debut in *Hamlet*, 1767; quoted in Michael Billington, *The Guinness Book of Theatre Facts and Feats*, 1982

In Maeterlinck's *The Blue Bird* I played the cat ... my entrance ... I made as big as I could, naturally, with the immortal line, 'Mee-ow-you'. – **Rex Harrison** *Rex*, 1974

Actors cannot choose the manner in which they are born – consequently it is the one gesture in their lives completely devoid of self-consciousness. – **Helen Hayes** *On Reflection*, 1968

I had no real ambition about acting, but I knew there had to be something better than the bloody chemist's shop.
– **Glenda Jackson** who started working life at Boot's the Chemist

I thought all acting was making love in tights to pretty women, and I determined to devote my life to it. – **Jerome K. Jerome** *On the Stage and Off*, 1885

There comes a time in everyone's life when he feels he was born to be an actor ... This sort of thing generally takes a man when he is about nineteen and lasts till he is nearly twenty. But he doesn't know this at the time. – Ibid.

I know mum and dad do not want me to act and think that I won't. BUT I WILL.
– **Alec McCowen** diary entry, aged 13, *Sunday Times*, 19 January 1992

One went to school, one wanted to act, one started to act and one is still acting.
– **Maggie Smith**

The small boy who played Brutus is already a great actor.

– **Ellen Terry** on Laurence Olivier, diary entry December 1916, after seeing the 9-year-old Olivier in a school play at All Saints School, Marylebone

I learned two things at RADA: first, that I couldn't act; second, that it didn't matter.

– **Wilfred Hyde White**

SARAH BERNHARDT

(ON HERSELF)
I loved many people, many things. But all I can remember now is that I loved the stage. Write of me only that please, young reporter, that I loved the stage.

– **Sarah Bernhardt** quoted in Ben Hecht, *A Child of the Century*, 1923

(BY OTHERS)
She is a bit of smoke, a breath of mist – a fugitive vision of delicate features under a shower of hair and a cloud of lace.

– **Anonymous critic** 1868 in H. and D. L. Thomas, *Living Biographies of Famous Women*; quoted in F. S. Pepper, *Dictionary of Biographical Quotations*, 1985

She has the head of a virgin and the body of a broomstick.

– **Alexandre Dumas** 1865

The most remarkable phenomenon of the 19th century.

– **Edmond de Goncourt**

You are too stupid to be much of an actress, but it will keep you out of mischief. – **Julie von Hard**, Bernhardt's mother, when Bernhardt started her training

A great actress from the waist down. – **Madge Kendal** quoted by Brooks Atkinson, *New York Times Book Review*, 25 May 1969

She was morbid to the point of artistic passion. She fell deeply in love with an undertaker's assistant but refused to marry him when he would not permit her to be present at an embalming. Between the hours of her rehearsals she visited the cemeteries of Paris and sat among the tombstones like a sister of the departed.

– **H. and D. L. Thomas** *Living Biographies of Famous Women*

It has been said that she died in harness. That expression of a plodder overtaken by death is inadequate for so gallant, so defiantly twinkling an exit. She was a boat that went to the bottom with its orchestra playing gaily.

– **Alexander Woollcott** *Enchanted Aisles*, 1924

BILLING

I'm now quite glad my name is Hermione Gingold because it's such a long name that on theatre billboards there isn't room for another name beside it.

– **Hermione Gingold** *How to Grow Old Disgracefully*, 1989

BROADWAY

'The Great White Way'
'The Street of the Midnight Sun'
Broadway – a branch of the narcotics world run by actors.

– **Bertolt Brecht**

What a glorious garden of wonders the lights would be to anyone lucky enough to be unable to read.

– **G. K. Chesterton** *What I Saw in America*, 1923

When you leave New York you're camping out.

– **Nat Goodwin**

Broadway is like a powerful magnet, with a pull that is overwhelming.

· **Mary Martin** quoted in D. Richards, *The Curtain Rises*, 1966

In 42nd Street it is a glowing summer afternoon all night: one might almost wear white trousers and a straw hat.

– **Paul Morand** quoted in B. Atkinson, *Broadway*, 1970

I read Shakespeare very well.

Variety I still cannot read.
– **Maurice Pagnol**
commenting on the unique
'showbiz' language of *Variety*

Since Mr [Charles] Dickens'
time the pigs of Broadway
have changed only in
form, having taken on the
semblance of humans. You
can see them today in the
streetcars and subway trains,
pushing and grunting their
way to seats while women
stand clinging to the straps.
You can see them wandering
along Broadway, old hogs
familiar with every sty in the
city, and young porkers just
learning the ways of swine,
their little eyes eagerly
watching every passing skirt.

Of an evening they gather
in cabarets, wallowing in
illicit liquor and shouting
through a conversational
garbage made up of oaths
and filthy stories and
scandal.

A pig is a pig even when it
wears evening clothes . . .
– **Damon Runyan**

The hardened artery.
– **Walter Winchell**

As far as Broadway is
concerned, a star that is no
longer in the ascendant is
already extinct.
– **Walter Winchell**

MRS PATRICK CAMPBELL

(ON HERSELF)
I look like a burst paper bag.
. . . I must borrow a chair
with a high back so that I
can hide my chins behind it.
– **Mrs Patrick Campbell**

(BY OTHERS)
The Lord Mayor's coach
with nothing inside it.
– **James Agate** on Mrs
Campbell as Mrs Alving in
Ibsen's *Ghosts*

The best tragic or emotional
actress in the country. In the
sheer acting sense, by which
one means the marriage
of spirit and the technical
means to convey that spirit,
Mrs Campbell has no rival
on our stage. – **James Agate**
1928; review of Mrs Patrick
Campbell as Ella Rentheim
in *John Gabriel Borkman*

Her voice was like Casals' cello and her silences had the emotional significance of Maeterlinck's shadowy speech.
– **James Agate** quoted in *Bernard Shaw and Mrs Patrick Campbell: Their Correspondence* (ed. Alan Dent), 1952

This was an actress who, for twenty years had the world at her feet. She kicked it away, and the ball rolled out of her reach. – Ibid.

On one occasion after a particularly wild 'tantrum' she walked to the footlights and peered out at Yeats, who was pacing up and down the stalls of the Abbey Theatre. 'I'd give anything to know what you're thinking,' shouted Mrs Pat. 'I'm thinking', replied Yeats, 'of the master of a wayside Indian railway station who sent a message to his Company's headquarters saying: "Tigress on the line: wire instructions."'
– **Gabriel Fallon** *Sean O'Casey: The Man I Knew*

As for the final stabbing scene, she might as well have tickled herself with a straw and died o' laughing.
– *Punch* review of Mrs Patrick Campbell as Juliet in *Romeo and Juliet*, 1895

It is greatly to Mrs Patrick Campbell's credit that, bad as the play was, her acting was worse.
– **George Bernard Shaw** reviewing *Fedora*, 1895

You will tell me that Mrs Patrick Campbell cannot act. Who said she could? – Who wants her to act? – Who cares tuppence whether she possesses that or any other second-rate accomplishment? On the highest plane one does not act, one is. Go and see her move, stand, look, kneel – go and breathe the magic atmosphere that is created by the grace of all those deeds; and then talk to me about acting, forsooth! – **George Bernard Shaw** *Saturday Review*, 7 March 1896

Bah! You have no nerve, you have no brain: you are the

caricature of an 18th-century male sentimentalist, a Hedda Gabler titivated with odds and ends from Burne-Jones' rag-bag. You are an owl sickened by two days of my sunshine.
– **George Bernard Shaw** 1913

If only you could write a book entitled WHY, THOUGH I WAS A WONDERFUL ACTRESS, NO MANAGER OR AUTHOR WOULD EVER ENGAGE ME TWICE IF HE COULD POSSIBLY HELP IT, it would be a best-seller. But you couldn't. Besides, you don't know. I do.
– **George Bernard Shaw** letter 19 December 1938; *Bernard Shaw and Mrs Patrick Campbell: Their Correspondence* (ed. Alan Dent), 1952. Shaw and Mrs Patrick Campbell enjoyed a correspondence over many years but the letters ceased after her persistent attempts to persuade him to allow these private letters to be published.

In the acting of women with brains and with natures complex, strange or highly strung she had not her equal on the English stage.
– *The Times* obituary, 1940

She was a sinking ship firing upon her rescuers.
– **Alexander Woollcott** *While Rome Bums*, 1934

An ego like a raging tooth.
– **W. B. Yeats** quoted in Gabriel Fallon, *Sean O'Casey: The Man I Knew*

CENSORSHIP

Nothing is unacceptable on stage except the breakdown of communication.
– **Howard Barker** quoted in *Contemporary Dramatists*, 1977

The result of the rehearsal is that H.M. thinks I had better not call her daughter 'a degraded woman', and I agree! Also she is not to say to Sir C. in describing her wooing of Clutterbuck, 'I have nothing to offer as dowry but my virtue', to which C. replies, 'Ah, little enough'. – **Arthur Bigge** describing some difficulties arising during an amateur production of *L'Homme Blasé* with Princess Louise, daughter of Queen Victoria (H.M.)

I acknowledge Shakespeare to be the world's greatest dramatic poet, but regret that no parent could place the uncorrected book in the hands of his daughter, and therefore I have prepared the Family Shakespeare.
– **Thomas Bowdler** preface to Thomas and Harriet Bowdler's expurgated edition, *The Family Shakespeare*, 1818

Nothing is added to the original text, but those words and expressions are omitted which cannot with propriety be read aloud in a family. – Ibid.

I think sex should be done, but unlike justice, not seen to be done. – **Evelyn Laye** quoted in D. Richards, *The Curtain Rises*, 1966

Requirement: Jack and Deirdre must sit on the bed as allowed. They may not lie. Jack must be fully clothed, not in déshabillé, and Deirdre's slip must be inside her breeches.
– **The Lord Chamberlain** on John Osborne's play *The World of Paul Slickey*; quoted in G. Snell, *The Book of Theatre Quotes*, 1982

If the theatre were to be shut up, the stage wholly silenced and suppressed, I believe the world, bad as it is now, would be ten times more wicked. – **Antoine Houdar de la Motto**

Christians must not lift up their eyes to stage plays, the pleasurable delights of polluted eyes, lest their lusts be inflamed by them.
– **Origen** 3rd century AD

The first condition of progress is the abolition of censorship.
– **George Bernard Shaw**

What matters is not what the censor does to what I have written, but to what I might have written. – **Leo Tolstoy**

CHARITY GALAS

*We're going to do a Midnight
    Matinée!
We're going to do a Midnight
    Show!
We're not quite sure
What charity it's for
But probably the Press will
    know...*
– **Noël Coward** 'Midnight
Matinée' (song); *The Lyrics
of Noël Coward*, 1965

CHEKHOV

Southern Fried Chekhov.
– Cast nickname for *The
Wisteria Tree*, Joshua Logan's
adaptation of *The Cherry
Orchard*, set in the deep
South

I hate plays that have a
stuffed bird sitting on the
book-case screaming,'I'm
the tide! I'm the tide! I'm the
title!'
– **Noël Coward** on
Chekhov's *The Seagull*

If you were to ask me what
Uncle Vanya is about, I
would say about as much as I
can take.

– **Robert Garland** review
of *Uncle Vanya* in *Journal
American* 1946

I cannot bear Shakespeare,
you know, but your plays are
even worse.
– **Leo Tolstoy** to Chekhov
quoted in M. Gorelick,
New Theatres for Old, 1940

CHILD ACTORS

Two things should be
cut – the second Act and
that child's throat. – **Noël
Coward** after seeing *Gypsy*
in London with its vivacious
child star Bonnie Langford

I was grown-up at ten, and
first began to grow young
at forty. – **Madge Kendal**
quoted in Alfred Miles, *The
New Anecdote Book*, 1906

CLUBS

The *Players* are all gentlemen
who wish they were actors.
The *Lambs* are all actors who
wish they were gentlemen.
The *Friars* wish they were
both. – **19th-century saying**

on New York's three best-known theatrical clubs

Member of the Garrick after a confrontation: When I joined, all the members were gentlemen. **Herbert Beerbohm Tree**: I wonder why they left?
– Quoted in Hesketh Pearson, *Beerbohm Tree*, 1956

COMEDY

Comedy aims at representing men as worse, and tragedy as better, than in real life.– **Aristotle** *Poetics II c.*322 AD

Nobody ever died of laughter. – **Max Beerbohm**

The powerful advantage of our theatrical tradition is that it is profoundly comic. Serious matters can be tackled in the theatre by mucking about and having some fun with what is meant to be unstageable.
– **Howard Brenton**

The most difficult character in comedy is that of a fool,

and he must be no simpleton who plays the part.
– **Cervantes** *Don Quixote*, 1605

Of all days, the day on which one has not laughed is surely the most wasted.
– **Chamfort** *Maximes et Pensées*, 1805

The whole of comedy depends on timing – and if you are really on your toes, you play the audience and you control the laughter.
– **Noël Coward**

All comedians are anarchists. – **Ken Dodd**

Comedy, like sodomy, is an unnatural act.
– **Marty Feldman** 1969

You may humbug the town as a tragedian, but comedy is a serious thing, my boy, so don't try that just yet.
– **David Garrick** to Jack Bannister; quoted in Laurence Hutton, *Curiosities of the American Stage*, 1891

Dying is easy. Comedy is hard. – **Edmund Kean**

I have noticed that in plays where the characters on stage laugh a great deal, the people out front laugh very little. – **Jean Kerr**

The debauching of virgins and the *amours* of strumpets are the subject of comedy. – **Lactantius** *Divinarum Institutionum VI c.310 AD*

A farce or a comedy is best played; a tragedy is best read at home. – **Abraham Lincoln** to John Hay after seeing Edwin Booth in *The Merchant of Venice* 1863 (Lincoln was assassinated by Booth's brother in 1865).

A comedian is not an actor. His work bears the same relation to acting as that of a hangman, a midwife, or a divorce lawyer bears to poetry, or that of a bishop to religion. – **G. L. Mencken** 1929

Comedy is the fountain of sound sense. – **George Meredith** *The Idea of Comedy*, 1877

1. Have I not been heard?

2. Was the line before mine not heard? 3. Was I truthful? – **Athene Seyler** (checklist after failing to get a laugh in the right place) *The Craft of Comedy* (with Stephen Haggard), 1944

Humour is like a frog – dissect it and it dies. – **Mark Twain**

Comedy is simply a funny way of being serious. – **Peter Ustinov**

Comedians; the second oldest profession which, like the first, has been ruined by amateurs. – **Ben Warriss** quoted in Simon Brett, *A Comedian Dies*, 1979

COSTUME AND MAKE-UP

Mr John Mills wanders around the stage at the St James Theatre looking like a bewildered carrot. – **Anonymous critic** on John Mills's red wig in *The Uninvited Guest*; quoted in D. Rigg, *No Turn Unstoned*, 1982

I am doing it for myself. If I catch sight of my hand it will be the hand of Cleopatra. That will help me.
– **Sarah Bernhardt** explaining her meticulous character make-up to Mrs Patrick Campbell; quoted in W. G. Robertson, *Life was Worth Living*, 1931

It's like looking out of a yak's arse! – **Coral Browne** on the wig for her part in *The Sea* by Edward Bond

I look like an elderly wasp in an interesting condition.
– **Mrs Patrick Campbell** on the black and yellow costume for her part as an Ancient Egyptian in *False Gods* 1909; quoted in R. May, *The Wit of the Theatre*, 1969

My attitude to make-up is the same as my attitude to directors – never use them.
– **Denholm Elliott** quoted at the London Theatre Museum exhibition on stage make-up, 1992

Curls, I think (pausing to pat her hair) – yes *curls*.
– **Edith Evans** 1954. After Christopher Fry had finished painstakingly reading her the whole of his new play, *The Dark is Light Enough*; recalled by Noel Davis

I love the fact that actors always go straight to their appearance. When Bully Bottom is given the part of Pyramus in *A Midsummer Night's Dream*, the first question he asks director Quince is: 'What beard were I best play it in?' There speaks the actor. – **Peter Hall** *Diaries*, 4 July 1972

You hear Macbeth's first line, then Larry's make-up comes on, then Banquo comes on, then Larry comes on. – **Vivien Leigh** commenting on Olivier's typically heavy stage make-up during the 1937 *Macbeth* at the Old Vic; quoted in A. Holden, *Olivier*, 1983

Twenty minutes for character make-up: ninety for a straight and, if you are playing a juvenile, wash your hair and fluff it up, and pinch your cheeks before you go on. – **Henry Livings** summary of theatre lore on make-up; quoted in R. May, *The Wit of the Theatre*, 1969

Oh yes, tired boy stuff, don't you dare remove it with your bloody retouching, old boy.
– **Laurence Olivier** 1937, to theatre photographer Angus McBean. McBean had remarked on his elaborate make-up for *Hamlet* which included painting the skin under his eyes white.

About wearing period costume; the most important thing is not the dress one wears but what one wears underneath it, and in one's mind.
– **Athene Seyler** *Fans, Trains and Stays* 1947 (reprinted in *The Craft of Comedy*, 1958)

Mrs Patrick Campbell's dresses, says the programme, carried out by Mrs Mason of New Burlington Street. I can only say that I wish they had been carried out and buried.
– **George Bernard Shaw** reviewing *Romeo and Juliet*, 1895

NOËL COWARD

(ON HIMSELF)
I am determined to travel through life first class.
My object in *The Vortex* was to write a good play with a whacking good part in it for myself.
– **Noël Coward** TV interview (USA) *c.*1956

I was photographed and interviewed and photographed again. In the street. In the park. In my dressing-room. At my piano. With my dear old mother. Without my dear old mother and on one occasion sitting up in an over-elaborate bed looking like a heavily doped Chinese illusionist.
– **Noël Coward** on the reaction to his play *Easy Virtue*, 1926; *Present Indicative*, 1937

Why am I always expected to wear a dressing gown, smoke cigarettes in a long holder and say 'Darling, how wonderful'?– **Noël Coward**

The critics described *Private Lives* variously as 'tenuous,

thin, brittle, gossamer, iridescent and delightfully daring'. All of which connotated in the public mind cocktails, repartee, and irreverent allusions to copulation, thereby causing a gratifying number of respectable people to queue up at the box office.
– **Noël Coward** *Present Indicative*, 1937

The day I shall begin to worry is when the critics declare, 'This is Noël Coward's greatest play.' But I know they bloody well won't. – **Noël Coward**

Oh, you know. Jack of all trades, master of none.
– **Noël Coward** *Sunday Mirror*, on the reason for his nick-name The Master, quoted in D. Richards, *The Wit of Noël Coward*

A definition of a genius is anyone from England.
– **Noël Coward** quoted by Daniel Massey, BBC TV interview, 1 March 1992

A lot of people said what a pity that I wasn't more

significant. That never worried me because I didn't really particularly wish to be significant. I'd like to be contemporary and bright as a button, but I don't think I was all that keen on being significant. – **Noël Coward** TV interview, 1969

I was trained very young as a show-off – and I've continued triumphantly to this moment. – **Noël Coward** TV interview, 1969

(BY OTHERS)
A dustbin of a play.
– **Anonymous critic** on Coward's play about drug-abuse, *The Vortex*, 1924

Your characters talk like typewriting and you yourself talk like a telegram. – **Mrs Patrick Campbell** on the first night of *The Vortex*, 1924

One can't read any of Noël Coward's plays now, they are written in the most topical and perishable way imaginable, the cream in them turns sour overnight.
– **Cyril Connolly** 1937

Noël Coward is a busy and talented young man, but when it comes to acting I believe he belongs in the will-power class. His notion of acting is to hold his body rigid and bite out cutting remarks.
– **Don Herold**

'I'm richly gifted and highly talented' – that was the phrase he used. It didn't seem arrogant with him, but he used it an awful lot.
– **Daniel Massey** BBC TV interview, 1 March 1992

Could I write as witty
As Noël Coward
By self-esteem
I should be devoward.
– **Ogden Nash** 'Encyclopedia Britannica', *New Yorker*, 23 May 1931

He apparently has nothing any longer to sell us but his own vast personal boredom.
– **George Jean Nathan** *Encyclopaedia of the Theatre*, 1940

He was his own greatest invention. – **John Osborne** quoted in William Marchant, *The Pleasure of His Company*

The First Noel.
–**Dick Richards** *The Curtain Rises*, 1966

If you wish to see him full-length, you must wait for his cabaret appearances. In these he is benign, though slightly flustered, as a cardinal might be who has been asked to participate in a frenetic tribal rite.
– **Kenneth Tynan** *Persona Grata*, 1953

Gracious socially as a royal bastard; tart, vocally, as a hollowed lemon – these are the signs by which we recognise him. – Ibid.

Forty years ago he was Slightly in *Peter Pan*, and you might say he's been wholly in *Peter Pan* ever since. – **Kenneth Tynan**, *Curtains*, 1961

If his face suggested an old boot it was unquestionably hand-made.
– **Kenneth Tynan** *The Sound of Two Hands Clapping*, 1975

CRITICAL ABUSE – ACTORS

MADGE BRINDLEY
Miss Lummins, as Miss Madge Brindley presents her, is straight out of Rowlandson, and she has a deadly aim with her saliva.
– **Roger Spate** reviewing *A Dead Secret* in the *New Statesman*, 1957

RICHARD BURTON
You may be as vicious about me as you please. You will only do me justice.
– **Richard Burton** on himself *New York Times*, 25 July 1978

CRESTON CLARKE
Last night Mr Creston Clarke played King Lear at the Tabor Grand. All through the five acts of that Shakespearean tragedy he played the King as though under momentary apprehension that someone else was about to play the Ace.
– **Eugene Field** review in *Denver Tribune*, c.1880

CHARLES COCHRAN
Charles B. Cochran played the part of Smart the detective. He certainly must have learned the art of acting in a stable with hungry horses; he did nothing but attempt to chew the paint from the scenery. A more ridiculous chump has never been seen on the stage.
– **Pennsylvania newspaper** reviewing the future impresario

MARION DAVIES
She has two expressions – joy and indigestion.
– **Dorothy Parker**

ELEONORA DUSE
However, it was not the only performance of Hedda Gabler. There was another and, in some ways a better. While Signora Duse walked through her part, the prompter threw himself into it with a will. A more raucous whisper I never heard than that which preceded the Signora's every sentence. It was like the continuous tearing of very thick silk.
– **Max Beerbohm** on Eleonora Duse's *Hedda Gabler* in *Saturday Review*

ROBERT ELLISTON

A wretched Tragedian . . . his attempts at dignity are ludicrous. He is a fine bustling comedian but he bustles in tragedy too.
– **Henry C. Robinson** *Diary*, 1811

SAMUEL FOOTE

On a Pseudo Player

Thou Mimic of Cibber – of
*   Garrick, thou Ape!*
Thou Fop in Othello/ Thou
*   Cypher in Shape!*
Thou Trifle in Person! Thou
*   Puppet in Voice!*
Thou Farce of a Player! Thou
*   Rattle for Boys!*
Thou Mongrell! Thou dirty
*   face Harlequin Thing!*
Thou Puff of bad Paste! Thou
*   Ginger-bread King!*

– **Anonymous** poem on the 18th-century actor Samuel Foote; quoted in W. T. Chetwood, *A General History of the Stage*

RUTH GORDON

Ruth Gordon plays Lola Pratt, and anyone who looks like that and acts like that must get off the stage.
– **Heywood C. Broun**

It is a generous role for womanly and impassioned actresses, and many performers have essayed it. I can think of four however, who have not: Totie Edwards, W. C. Fields, Tutankhamen's mummy, and a trained monkey. Not until now that is; Miss Gordon's performance combines elements of all four. – **John Simon** reviewing Shaw's *Mrs Warren's Profession*

CEDRIC HARDWICKE

He conducted the soul-selling transaction with the thoughtful dignity of a grocer selling a pound of cheese. – **Hubert Griffith** reviewing Cedric Hardwicke as Marlowe's *Dr Faustus*, *Sunday Graphic*, September 1948; quoted in D. Rigg, *No Turn Unstoned*, 1982

HELEN HAYES

Miss Hayes is not, in my minority opinion, one of the world's most gifted performers. – **Tennessee Williams** on the 'first lady' of American theatre

Fallen archness.
– **Franklin Pierce Adams** on Helen Hayes as Cleopatra in Shaw's *Caesar and Cleopatra*, 1925

KATHERINE HEPBURN
She ran the gamut of emotions all the way from A to B. – **Dorothy Parker** on Hepburn's performance in *The Lake*, 1933

MICHAEL HORDERN
Michael Hordern's Cassius has an anxious air. This Cassius watches John Phillips' alarmingly tall Brutus like an insurance agent estimating how much life cover he can offer without insisting on a medical examination.
– *Sunday Times* review of *Julius Caesar*, October 1958; quoted in D. Rigg, *No Turn Unstoned*, 1982

CHARLES LAUGHTON
Mr Laughton came to Sadlers Wells with all his blushing film vulgarities thick upon him.
– **James Agate** on Charles Laughton in *Henry VIII*, 1933

GERTRUDE LAWRENCE
A bad play saved by a bad performance.
– **George S. Kaufman** reviewing Gertrude Lawrence in *Skylark*

MOIRA LISTER
Miss Moira Lister speaks all her lines as if they are written in very faint ink on a tele-prompter slightly too far away to be read with comfort.
– **Bernard Levin** on *The Gazebo* in the *Daily Express*, 1960

MONTAGUE LOVE
Mr Love's idea of playing a he-man was to extend his chest three inches and then follow it slowly across the stage. – **Heywood C. Broun** 1921; quoted in A. Woollcott, *Enchanted Aisles*, 1924

FREDERIC MARCH
He came in like a lion and went out like a ham.
– **Frank Nugent** reviewing Frederic March in *The Buccaneer*, 1958

RAYMOND MASSEY
Massey won't be satisfied

until he's assassinated.
– **George S. Kaufman** 1938;
reviewing *Abe Lincoln in Illinois*

GERALDINE MCEWAN
Geraldine McEwan, powdered white like a clownish, whey-faced doll, simpered, whined and groaned to such an effect as the Queen, that Edward's homosexuality became both understandable and forgivable.
– **Milton Shulman** reviewing Marlowe's *Edward II*, 1968

A. E. MATTHEWS
A. E. Matthews ambled through *This Was a Man* like a charming retriever who has buried a bone and can't remember where.
– **Noël Coward** 1926

GUIDO NADZO
Guido Nadzo is nadzo guido.
– **George S. Kaufman** on a little known American actor

ANNA NEAGLE
Her Victoria made me feel that Albert had married beneath his station.

– **Noël Coward** attrib. after seeing *Victoria Regina*

PETER O'TOOLE
He delivers every line with a monotonous tenor bark as if addressing an audience of deaf eskimos.
– **Michael Billington** on O'Toole's notorious *Macbeth* in *The Guardian*, 1980

DENIS QUILLEY
Denis Quilley played the role with all the charm and animation of the leg of a billiard table.
– **Bernard Levin** reviewing *High Spirits*, the musical version of Coward's *Blithe Spirit* 1965

JAY ROBINSON
Mr Robinson was game all right. But what is gameness in a man who is suffering from delusions of adequacy?
– **Walter Kerr** reviewing Jay Robinson (who was also the producer) in *Buy Me Blue Ribbons*, 1951

PAUL SCOFIELD
His playing bores the doublet and hose off me.
– **Bernard Levin** on Paul

Scofield as Thomas More in Robert Bolt's *A Man for All Seasons* in the *Daily Express*, 1960

Mr Yorke Stephens fulfills his obligations to Miss Corelli and the audience most scrupulously but with the air of a man who has resolved to shoot himself the moment the curtain has come down.
– **George Bernard Shaw** reviewing *The Sorrows of Satan* by Marie Corelli in the *Saturday Review*, 1897

Mr Steyn's performance was the worst to be seen in the contemporary theatre.
– **Heywood C. Broun** on American actor Geoffrey Steyn, 1917. Mr Steyn sued Heywood Broun. During the litigation Steyn appeared in another play which prompted the following carefully worded appraisal from Broun: 'Mr Steyn's performance is not up to his usual standard.'

Elizabeth Taylor's performance hardly carries into the auditorium. Ambrose Hammer – a critic who loves to heave the harpoon into actors might carry on from there. I merely say that the first night . . . is as grisly as an undertaker's picnic and may be grislier.
– **Robert Cushman** reviewing Elizabeth Taylor's performance in Lillian Hellman's *The Little Foxes* in the *Observer*, 1982

As swashbuckling Cyrano, Mr Woodward's performance buckles more often than it swashes.
– **Kenneth Hurran** reviewing Edward Woodward in Rostand's *Cyrano de Bergerac* in the *Spectator*, 1970

Too much stumping about and too much flumping about.
– **Kitty Clive** quoted in W. Clark Russell, *Representative Actors*

CRITICAL ABUSE – PLAYS

UN-NAMED PLAYS
(Listed alphabetically by reviewer)

Rainstorm in Galveston, lasted twenty minutes. Hail storm in Beaumont, ten minutes. Wind storm in Langtry, two days. Barn storm in Opera house, one night. – **Anonymous** review of a touring show in local paper, Waco, Texas quoted in *The Wit and Humour of the Stage*, 1909

Methought this was addressed to me. Metook the hint. – **James Agate** reviewing a play in which the line 'Methinks you did wrong to come' occurs

It opened at 8.40 sharp and closed at 10.40 dull.
– **Heywood C. Broun** attrib.

The Messrs. Shubert seem to forget that the female knee is a joint and not an evening's entertainment.
– **Percy Hammond**

I have knocked everything in this play except the chorus girls' knees, and there God has anticipated me.
– **Percy Hammond**

Of the acting of Miss Berger's company one may not speak candidly unless one is in a trench.
– **Percy Hammond**

I saw the play at a disadvantage – the curtain was up.
– **George S. Kaufman** attrib. remark quoted in H. Teichmann, *George S. Kaufman: An Intimate Portrait*, 1972 (also attributed to **Groucho Marx**)

In Boston the test of a play is simple. If the play is bad the pigeons snarl at you as you walk across the common.
– **George S. Kaufman** quoted in H. Teichmann, *George S. Kaufman: An Intimate Portrait*, 1972

There was laughter at the back of the theatre, leading to the belief that someone was telling jokes back there.
– **George S. Kaufman**

The costumes looked as though they had been selected by Helen Keller.
– **George Jean Nathan** on a 1920s revue

The Greeks had a word for it – so did the Hebrews – lousy.
– **Dorothy Parker**

The best play I ever slept through. – **Oscar Wilde**

I've seen more excitement at the opening of an umbrella.
– **Earl Wilson**

The scenery was beautiful but the actors got in front of it.
–**Alexander Woollcott**

NAMED PLAYS
(Listed alphabetically by reviewer)

It is dramatized stench.
– **Anonymous** review of Shaw's *Mrs Warren's Profession*, 1898 (Mrs Warren operates a chain of brothels in Europe)

There were fifty in the cast and ten real bloodhounds. The dogs gave an excellent performance but received little support from the rest of the company.
– **Review** of *Uncle Tom's Cabin*, 1907; quoted in J. Aye, *Humour in the Theatre*, 1932

Globe Theatre. *Mr Symkin.* Good God. What piffle.
– Ibid.

When Mr Wilbur calls his play *Halfway to Hell* he underestimates the distance.
– **Brooks Atkinson** 1934

There's less to this than meets the eye.
– **Tallulah Bankhead** on *The Burgomaster of Stilemonde* by Belgian symbolist Maeterlinck; *Tallulah*, 1952

The sort of show that gives pornography a bad name.
– **Clive Barnes** on Kenneth Tynan's erotic revue *Oh! Calcutta*, 1970

One of those plays in which all of the actors unfortunately enunciated very clearly.
– **Robert Benchley** on *Perfectly Scandalous*, 1931

Hebrews 13:8.
– **Robert Benchley** on the highly sentimental and long-running Broadway hit *Abie's Irish Rose*, which he loathed. The Biblical reference reads 'Jesus Christ, the same yesterday, and today, and forever.'

Designed by Cleon Throckmorton from sketches by Santiago Ontanon of an old Spanish intestinal tract.
– **Robert Benchley** on *Bitter Oleander*, 1937

So cheap and offensive that it might serve to unite all the races of the world in a common hymn of hate.
– **Heywood C. Broun** on *Abie's Irish Rose*, 1927 (Robert Benchley's *bête noire*)

It is enough to make your flesh crawl – right out of the Ethel Barrymore Theatre.
– **John Chapman** on *Last Stop* in *New York Daily News*, 1944

Very good – but a month in the wrong country.
– **Noël Coward** 1956; after an Actors' Studio production of Turgenev's *A Month in the Country*

It was very close to the real thing – but it seemed to last twice as long and be just as noisy.
– **Noël Coward** to Lionel Bart after the opening of Bart's musical *Blitz*, 1962

Twice as long as *Parsifal* and half as funny.
– **Noël Coward** on the musical *Camelot*, 1960

There's nothing wrong with that show that shoving the child up the horse's arse won't cure. – **Noël Coward** on the musical version of *Gone With the Wind* at Drury Lane, starring 3-year-old Bonnie Langford. During the performance one of the horses had defecated heavily on the stage.

I didn't pay £3.50 just to see half-a-dozen acorns and a chipolata. – **Noël Coward** 1972; after seeing David Storey's *The Changing Room* in which most of the actors appear unclothed.

Good Fielding. No Hit.
– **Kyle Crichton** on a stage version of Fielding's *Tom Jones*

It is the kind of play . . . that one might enjoy more at a second hearing if only the first time through hadn't left one such a strong feeling that once is enough. – **W. H. Darlington** on *Rosencrantz and Guildenstem are Dead* by Tom Stoppard in the *Daily Telegraph*, April 1967

It is curious how incest, impotence, nymphomania, religious mania and real estate speculation can be so dull. – **Richard Findlater** on *Toys in the Attic* by Lillian Hellman in *Time and Tide*, 1960

More like a Henderson Seed Co. catalogue than an honest to living drama.
– **Gilbert W. Gabriel** on *Bitter Oleander* in *The World*, 1935

Odets, where is they sting?
– **Robert Garland** on Clifford Odets' play, *Clash by Night*, 194 1

Marks the beginning of the Sodom and Begorra school.
– **Lionel Hale** on the Irish playwright Lady Longford's play about homosexuality, *Anything but the Truth*, 1937

Boston liked *Follow the Girls*. Boston also likes baked beans. – **Irving Hoffman** *Hollywood Reporter*, 1944

We're sorry but it's not our cup of tee-hee.
– **Irving Hoffman** reviewing *Mrs January and Mr Ex* in *Hollywood Reporter*, 1944

Last night a play called *Pure as Snow* was produced at the Broad Street Theatre. It was not as pure as snow. – **H. J. Jennings** quoted in J. Aye, *Humour in the Theatre*, 1932

Hook 'n' Ladder is the sort of play that gives failure a bad name. – **Walter Kerr**, 1952

I think they've made a mistake. They've left the show in Detroit, or wherever it was last warming up, and brought in the publicity stills. – **Walter Kerr** reviewing *Ilya Darling*, 1967

I saw this show under adverse circumstances – my seat was facing the stage. – **John David Klein** on *Three Guys Naked from the Waist Down*, 1985

A woman's magazine romance that goes backwards until it disappears up its own pauses. – **Herbert Kretzmer** on Harold Pinter's *Betrayal* in the *Daily Express*, 1978

A dirty-minded little girl's essay on the Russian Empress, played like a chatelaine of an old time 'maison de joie'. – **Louis Kronenburger** on Mae West's *Catherine Was Great*, 1944

I'm afraid *The Intelligent Woman's Guide* I shall have to leave to the intelligent woman: it is too boring for the intelligent man, if I am any sample. Too much gas-bag. – **D. H. Lawrence** on Shaw's *The Intelligent Woman's Guide*, 1928

A lot of Chinese junk . . . In wise old Lee Vin's opinion, if you want more of China than wide sleeves, and more of a play than romantic twaddle, to pay it a visit would be to enter the world of choosy wrong. – **Bernard Levin** on *The World of Suzie Wong* in the *Daily Express* 1959

I think *The Amorous Prawn* is perhaps the most grisly, glassy eyed thing I have encountered in the theatre for a very long time, and even outside the theatre its like is rarely met except on fishmongers' slabs, and now I feel very ill indeed, and would like to lie down. Before doing so I should like to say that *The Amorous Prawn* is a farce made out of cobwebs and mothballs, my old socks, empty beer bottles, copies of the Strand Magazine, dust, holes, mildew and Mr Ben Travers' discarded typewriter ribbons. – **Bernard Levin** on *The Amorous Prawn* in the *Daily Express*, 1959

Strictly speaking I cannot swear that being kicked in the stomach by a horse

would be an experience preferable to seeing this play by Signor Giuseppe Marotti because I have never been kicked in the stomach by a horse. But I have seen this play, and I can certainly say that if a kick in the stomach by a horse would be worse, I do not wish to be kicked in the stomach by a horse. And I can certainly add that, unpleasant though the prospect of being kicked in the stomach by a horse may be, I would certainly rather be kicked in the stomach by a horse than see the play again.
– **Bernard Levin** on *Dazzling Prospect* in the *Daily Express*, 1961

I think I'll go by boat.
– **Bernard Levin** on Marc Camoletti's *Boeing Boeing* in the *Daily Express*, 1963

Why should I pay ten dollars to see something I can see in the bathroom for nothing?
– **Groucho Marx** on *Hair*, 1968

No worse than a bad cold.
– **Harpo Marx** on the saccharine sweet play *Abie's Irish Rose*, c.1929

The hills are alive with the sound of clichés. – **Sheridan Morley** on *Mistress of Novices*, *Punch*, 1973

There is a number of possible explanations for the presence of *Il Campiello* in the repertoire of the National Theatre at the Olivier. The one I like best is that it represents a complete and never-to-be-repeated mental, physical and theatrical breakdown on the part of all concerned.
– **Sheridan Morley** *Punch*, 1973

The majority of mystery plays, with their disappointing solutions, are like sitting nervously around for two hours waiting for a telephone call from one's best girl and then at long length suddenly hearing the bell ring, jumping up eagerly to answer it, and finding that it is her mother! This was no exception.
– **George Jean Nathan** on *The Cat Screams*, 1942

Very well then: I say Never.
– **George Jean Nathan** on
Tonight or Never, 1930

Bosh sprinkled with mystic
cologne. – **George Jean
Nathan** on T. S. Eliot's *The
Cocktail Party*, 1950

The frocks were charming.
– Review of *Fresh Fields* by
Ivor Novello 1933; quoted in
D. Rigg, *No Turn Unstoned*,
1982

It isn't what you might
call sunny. I went into
the Plymouth Theatre a
comparatively young woman
and I staggered out of it
three hours later, twenty
years older, haggard and
broken with suffering.
– **Dorothy Parker** on
Tolstoy's *Redemption* in
Vanity Fair, 1928

The House Beautiful is the
play lousy.
– **Dorothy Parker** *Life*, 1931

Now that you've got me
right down to it, the only
thing I didn't like about *The
Barretts of Wimpole Street*
was the play.

– **Dorothy Parker** *New
Yorker*, 1931

This is a play for people who
wash every day.
– **Billy Rose** on Shaw's
Heartbreak House

Two minutes of *Biarritz*
would reconcile a Trappist
monk to his monastery for
life. – **George Bernard Shaw**
on *Biarritz* by Jerome K.
Jerome, 1896

NO!
– **Hannan Swaffer** reviewing
Yes and No, 1938

I left the show feeling very
keen to get home to the
washing up. – **Irving Wardle**
reviewing *What's Got into
You* in *The Times*, 1981

If this play lasts overnight
it should not only be
considered a long run but a
revival as well.
– **Alexander Woollcott** on
The Lake (starring Katherine
Hepburn)

CRITICISM

Only two roles of dramatic criticism matter. One. Decide what the playwright was trying to do, and pronounce how well he has done it. Two. Determine whether the well-done thing was worth doing at all.
– **James Agate** *Ego 8*, 1945

Dramatic criticism has three functions. The first is to let the world know what the previous night's play has been about. There's no reason why a report of this kind should not be written by the same man who describes how in the afternoon he saw a man knocked down in Oxford Street trying to stop a runaway horse. The second function is to tell the public whether the new play is good, bad or indifferent. This means the critic must know his job. That is if you hold with my dictionary, which defines criticism as 'The art of judging with 'knowledge and propriety of the beauties and faults of art.' The third is to report

the theatre in terms of the art of writing.
– **James Agate** *Ego 9*, 1946

I find that when I dislike what I see on stage then I can be vastly amusing, but when I write about something I like, I find I am appallingly dull.
– **Max Beerbohm**

To many people dramatic criticism must seem like an attempt to tattoo soap bubbles.– **John Mason Brown** quoted in Frank Muir, *The Frank Muir Book*

I love criticism, just so long as it is unqualified praise.
– **Noël Coward**

I know how good I am but I do not know how bad I am.
– **W. S. Gilbert** (the reason he preferred hostile criticism to fulsome praise)

Venom from contented rattlesnakes. – **Percy Hammond** (definition of dramatic criticism)

You may scold a carpenter who has made you a bad

table, though you cannot make a table.
– **Samuel Johnson**

Berating someone for failing to achieve what they never set out to do is one of the most elementary gambits of criticism. – **John Osborne**
Almost a Gentleman, 1991

It does not follow that the right to criticize Shakespeare involves the power of writing better plays.
– **George Bernard Shaw**

Reviewing has one advantage over suicide; in suicide you take it out on yourself; in reviewing you take it out on other people.
– **George Bernard Shaw**

Ideal dramatic criticism is unqualified appreciation.
– **Oscar Wilde**

CRITICS

When a play is crashingly dull the critic has only two resources. One is sleep, in justification whereof I shall quote William Archer's

dictum that the first qualification for a dramatic critic is the capacity to sleep while sitting bolt upright.
– **James Agate** 1932

If Attila the Hun were alive today, he'd be a dramatic critic. – **Edward Albee** 1983

One of the first and most important things for a critic to learn is how to sleep undetected in the theatre.
– **William Archer**

The dramatic critic is like the clergyman – he stands in a favoured position, and however hard he may hit, the recipient of his blows is, for the most part, unable to strike back. – **John Aye**
Humour in the Theatre, 1932

Critics are like eunuchs in a harem. They're there every night, they see it done every night, they see how it should be done every night, but they can't do it themselves.
– **Brendan Behan**

Critics should be searched for certain adjectives at the door of the theatre.

Irreverent, probing and (above all) satirical. I would have all such adjectives left with their coats in the foyer, only to be redeemed when their notices are written.
– **Alan Bennett**

The critic cannot do his work without hurting; he resembles the dentist.
– **Eric Bentley** *What is Theatre*, 1956

At any London first night you'll see the critics creeping off to the pub half-way through Act III. Of course they pretend they have to catch the early editions.
– **Basil Boothroyd**

There are nowadays a sort of persons they call critics that, egad, have no more wit in them than so many hobby horses. – **George Villiers**, 2nd Duke of Buckingham *The Rehearsal*, 1671

To poison plays I see some where they sit,
Scattered like ratsbane, up and down the pit.
– **William Congreve** 1697

Critics never worry me unless they are right – but that does not often occur.
– **Noël Coward**

It's so unwise of critics to predict. One said he would eat his hat if it [Nude With Violin] ran in the West End. It is still running. Of course I will not stand over him while he masticates the hat.
– **Noël Coward** *Daily Mail* interview, 1957

Who notices when they meet a critic whose face is tense with pain? It is one of the marks of the profession.
– **Robertson Davies** *Murther and Walking Spirits*, 1991

There are very few critics who when given an egg of talent in their hands can resist crushing it. – **Peter Hall** *Diaries*, 14 July 1974

The critic is often an unsuccessful author, almost always an inferior one.
– **Leigh Hunt**

A critic is a legless man who teaches running.
– **Channing Pollock**

A drama critic is a man who leaves no turn unstoned.
– **George Bernard Shaw** *New York Times*, 1950

Reviewers must normally function as huff-and-puff artists blowing laggard theatre-goers stageward.
– **A. A. Milne**

The dramatic critic who is without prejudice is on the same plane with the General who does not believe in taking life.
– **George Jean Nathan** *Comedians All*

The better and more honest a critic you are, the fewer friends will eventually send flowers up to the funeral parlour.
– **George Jean Nathan**

Critics: those who would send Hedda Gabler to the Marriage Guidance Council.
– **John Osborne** *A Better Class of Person*, 1981

As for the little puny critics, who scatter their peevish strictures in private circles, and scribble at every author who has the eminence of being un-connected with them, as they are usually spleen-swoln from a vain idea of increasing their consequence, There will always be found a petulance and illiberality in their remarks which should place them as far beneath the notice of a gentleman, as their original dullness had sunk them from the level of the most unsuccessful author.
– **Richard Brinsley Sheridan** preface to *The Rivals*, 1775

You will not easily persuade me that there is no credit or importance in being at the head of a band of critics, who take upon them to decide for the whole town, whose opinion and patronage all writers solicit, and whose recommendation no manager dares refuse. (Mr Dangle)
– **Richard Brinsley Sheridan** *The Critic*, 1779

A man who knows the way but can't drive the car.
– **Kenneth Tynan** (definition of a critic) quoted in *New*

York Times Magazine, 9
January 1966

A good drama critic is
one who perceives what is
happening in the theatre
of his time. A great drama
critic is one who perceives
what is not happening.
– **Kenneth Tynan**

They search for ages for the
wrong word which, to give
them credit, they eventually
find. – **Peter Ustinov**

The critic leaves at curtain fall
To find in starting to review it,
He scarcely saw the play at all
For watching his reaction to it.
– **D. B. White** *Critic*

A newspaperman, whose
sweetheart ran away with
an actor.– **Walter Winchell**
(definition of a critic)

Has anybody seen a
dramatic critic in the day-
time? Of course not. They
come out after dark, up to
no good. – **P. G. Wodehouse**
New York Mirror, 1955

CRITICS
– Personalities

CLIVE BARNES
It seems to me that giving
Clive Barnes his CBE for
services to the theatre is like
giving Goering the DFC for
services to the RAF.
– **Alan Bennett**

If I decide to stay around
Broadway beyond the
current season, it will be for
the pleasure of throwing his
fat, limey posterior out in
the street.
– **David Merrick**

MAX BEERBOHM
The gods bestowed on Max
the gift of perpetual old age.
– **Oscar Wilde**

ROBERT BENCHLEY
(ON HIMSELF)
I do most of my work sitting
down; that's where I shine.

It took me fifteen years to
discover I had no talent for
writing, but I couldn't give
it up because by that time I
was too famous.

HAZLITT

Hazlitt . . . had perhaps the most uninteresting mind of all our distinguished critics.
– **T. S. Eliot** *Essays: Dryden*

GEORGE JEAN NATHAN
(ON HIMSELF)

There are two kinds of dramatic critics: destructive and constructive. I am destructive. There are two kinds of guns: Krupp and pop. – *The World in False Face*, 1923

I hit upon dramatic criticism as a way to live luxuriously without too much brain exercise.
– *Encyclopaedia of the Theatre*, 1940

DOROTHY PARKER
(ON HERSELF)

Ducking for apples – change a letter and it's the story of my life.

I was the toast of two continents: Greenland and Australia.
– Quoted in J. Keats, *You Might As Well Live: Life and Times of Dorothy Parker*, 1970

(BY OTHERS)

Discussing a job with a prospective employer Mrs Parker explained 'Salary is no object. I only want enough to keep body and soul apart.'
– **Robert E. Brennan** *Wits End*

You see, she is so odd a blend of Little Nell and Lady Macbeth. It is not so much the familiar phenomenon of a hand of steel in a velvet glove as a lacy sleeve with a bottle of vitriol concealed in its folds.
– **Alexander Woollcott** *While Rome Burns*, 1934

KENNETH TYNAN

The sheer complexity of writing a play always had dazzled me. In an effort to understand it, I became a critic. – On himself *New York Mirror*, 1963

Quite dreadful, he would not get a chance in a village hall unless he were related to the vicar.
– **Beverley Baxter** on Tynan as First Player in the Alec Guinness *Hamlet*, 1951

He understood the buzz of actors' energy with a good text. – **William Dudley** December 1991

ALEXANDER WOOLLCOTT
(ON HIMSELF)
All the things I really like to do are either immoral, illegal or fattening.
– Woollcott was the originator of this widely quoted remark.

The thing's a terrible insult and I've decided to swallow it. – On George S. Kaufman's thinly disguised portrayal of him in *The Man Who Came to Dinner*, 1939

(BY OTHERS)
He was vindictive, shockingly petty, in a feminine fashion, given to excesses when expressing his preferences or his prejudices.
– **Tallulah Bankhead** *Tallulah*, 1952

His entrances down the aisles of New York theatres were more dramatic than most of the shows he reviewed.
– **John Mason Brown** *The Portable Woollcott*, 1946

His life was what the marquees describe as a 'continuous performance'.
– Ibid.

Alexander Woollcott, in a rage, has all the tenderness and restraint of a newly caged cobra. – **Noël Coward**

The New Jersey Nero who mistakes his pinafore for a toga.
– **Edna Ferber** attrib. *c*.1934

A striking combination of hero-worshipper and Madame Defarge.
– **Margaret Case Harriman** *The Vicious Circle*, 1951

I blame Alexander Woollcott and Robert Benchley and Dorothy Parker for parenting the cutesy and cruel critics who carve up the theatre we know now.
– **Mercedes McCambridge**

No-one writing about the theatre in his time was as provocative, or brought as much gusto and excitement to his subject. His emotions overrode his judgement, making his hates and

enthusiasms superlative.
– **Brock Pemberton** quoted in Samuel H. Adams, *A. Woollcott; His Life and His World*, 1945

The clowning blunder of my life.
– **Carr Van Anda** on hiring Woollcott as drama critic of the *New York Times*, quoted in S. H. Adams, *A. Woollcott; His Life and His World*, 1945

He always praises the first show of the season, being reluctant to stone the first cast.
– **Walter Winchell** quoted in S. H. Adams, *A. Woollcott; His Life and His World*, 1945

DEDICATION

Always a man to keep everything in proportion so long as the theatre was on top, Mr Langner remarked after the Armistice (1918) that he was glad the war was over because he wanted to organise another theatre.
– **Brooks Atkinson** on Lawrence Langner in *Broadway*, 1970

This lady was so very natural an actress, and was so powerfully affected by her feelings, that she seldom retired from any great tragic part without being in some degree affected by a stomachic complaint.
– **William Cook** on 18th-century actress Hannah Pritchard, *Memoirs of Samuel Foote*, 1805

I hate this new solemnity in the theatre. If anybody says to me 'She's a dedicated actress' I'd like to strangle her. What is she dedicated about?
– **Noël Coward**

Why must the show go on?
The rule is surely not
    immutable,
It might be wiser and more
    suitable
Just to close
If you are in the throes
Of personal grief and private
    woes.
– **Noël Coward** 'Why Must the Show Go On?' (song); *The Lyrics of Noël Coward*, 1965

Never at any time have I

gone on the stage without longing for the moment when the curtain would come down on the last act.
– **Sir Johnstone Forbes-Robertson** (who would rather have been a painter); quoted in Hesketh Pearson, *The Last Actor-Managers*, 1950

Actors playing with her these days whispered that as she gave her final death shriek in the part [Meg Merrilees], she pounded her breast, which was known to be on fire with cancer, so as to make her cry one of real agony. – **Eleanor Ruggles** on Charlotte Cushman in *Prince of Players: Edwin Booth*

I want to retire to a faraway desert island, a beautiful desert island, with a stretch of sea and sand and moonlight – just enough to read *Variety* by.
– **Lilian Tashman** quoted in Maurice Zolotov, *No People Like Show People*, 1951

When I'm acting I sometimes want to get my performance, put it through the mincer,

chuck it down the sink and start all over again.
– **Billie Whitelaw** *Daily Mail*, 13 June 1992

DIRECTORS

Theatre director . . . a person engaged by the management to conceal the fact that the players cannot act.
– **James Agate** *Sunday Times*

Theatre consists of two great arts: acting and playwriting; and there is no third art necessary to coordinate them.
– **James Agate** quoted in W. Redfield, *Letters from an Actor* 1967

A director has but one task: to make each rehearsal so amusing that the actors will look forward to the next one.
– **Martin Esslin** quoted in P. Hay, *Theatrical Anecdotes* 1987

All you can do with Shaw is to fan the actors out in a semi-circle, put the speaker at the top, and hope for the best.

– **Tyrone Guthrie** quoted in
A. Ross, *Astonish Us in the
Morning: Tyrone Guthrie
Remembered*, 1977

It is almost impossible
to make any form of
art without totalitarian
behaviour.
– **Peter Hall** *Diaries*,
28 April 1978

In the theatre the director is
God – but unfortunately the
actors are atheists.
– **Zarco Petan** *The Times*,
15 June 1977

The only time he [the
director] is of any use to me
is if I've left my script in the
car, and he volunteers to
fetch it.
– **Wilfred Hyde White**
quoted in R. May, *The Wit of
the Theatre*, 1969

DIRECTORS
– Individuals

PETER BROOK
I can take any empty space
and call it a bare stage.
– **Peter Brook** *The Empty
Space*, 1968

When we talk in Britain
these days of a director as
a creative genius . . . we are
almost invariably talking of
a foreigner . . . Peter Brook
is the only British man of
the theatre for whom such
a claim can confidently be
made . . . Brook is someone
prepared to take risks, fail
and then try again, succeed
and then try again: a genius,
and a creative one.
– **Benedict Nightingale** *The
Times Literary Supplement*

GEORGE DEVINE
He suffered talent gladly.
– **John Osborne** quoted in
R. Findlater, *At The Royal
Court*, 1981

PETER HALL
(ON HIMSELF)
I really work for the author
and a good rehearsal –
something which extends
the actors and myself.
– *Diaries*, 18 June 1972

There is nothing worse for
a director than the first day.
Much worse than the first
night.
– *Diaries*, 2 January 1974

The trouble with God is he thinks he's Peter Hall.
– **Graffito** on the walls of the National Theatre, 1970s

I do wish he'd stop pretending to be so bloody nice, when he's really a dictator.
– **Glenda Jackson** quoted in *The Times*, 20 June 1992

See also: Herbert Beerbohm Tree

DRESSING ROOM TALK

No matter how bad this is, I'm going to tell the poor boy I like it.
– **father** at the opening of *Silent Night, Lonely Night*, New York, 1959

Gushing visitor who had just seen **John Barrymore** play Hamlet: Oh Master! I enjoyed your performance so much.
John Barrymore: Not half as much as I'm enjoying yours.

Boy were you on that stage!
– **Diahann Carroll**
catch-all phrase for those embarrassing moments when you have to find something positive to say about the performance you have just witnessed

OTHER USEFUL EXCLAMATIONS INCLUDE:

My dear, unbelievable!
– **Noël Coward**

My dear chap! Good isn't the word! – **W. S. Gilbert**

And *what* about *you* then?
– **George Hall** (recalled by Selina Cadell)

Well, nobody got hurt.
– **Richard Maney** quoted in W. Redfield, *Letters from an Actor*

ELEONORA DUSE

Her features have the placidity of long grief; so many storms have broken over them that nothing can disturb again this sea of calm distress. – **James Agate**

She acted from the head
down, not from the feet
up. Her body was eloquent
because her legs had less to
do with manipulating it and
guiding it than her brain . . .
– **George Jean Nathan**
Materia Critica, 1924

The extended right arm
of Eleonora Duse had in it
all the tears of Tristan and
Isolde. – Ibid.

No physical charm is noble
as well as beautiful unless it
is the expression of a moral
charm; and it is because
Duse's range includes these
high moral notes that her
compass, extending from the
depths of a mere predatory
creature like Claude's wife
up to Marguerite Gautier at
her kindest or Magda at her
bravest, so dwarfs the poor
little octave and a half on
which Sarah Bernhardt plays
such pretty canzonets and
stirring marches.
– **George Bernard Shaw**
quoted in M. Billington, *The
Guinness Book of Theatre
Facts and Feats*, 1982

EPILOGUES

If it be true that good wine
    needs no bush,
'Tis true that a good play
    needs no epilogue.
– **William Shakespeare**
Epilogue of *As You Like It*

Catherine had three
hundred lovers. I did the
best I could in a couple of
hours.
– **Mae West** curtain speech
of her play *Catherine Was
Great*, 1944

EPITAPHS

Her name cut clear upon
    this marble cross,
Shines as it shone when she
    was still on earth,
While tenderly the mild,
    agreeable moss
Obscures the figures of her
    date of birth.
– **Dorothy Parker** tombstone
of an actress from
Tombstones in the Starlight

Good my lord, will you see
the players well bestowed?
Do you hear, let them be
well used; for they are the

abstract and brief chronicles of the time: after your death you were better have a bad epitaph than their ill report while you live.
– **William Shakespeare** *Hamlet*, Act III, Scene 2

EPITAPHS
– Individuals

LIONEL BARRYMORE
He played everything but a harp. – **Lionel Barrymore** suggestion for his own epitaph

GEORGINA DREW BARRYMORE
It's a cruel loss and I shall never get over it. But I must say they've given the old girl some damn good notices.
– **Maurice Barrymore** on the obituaries for his wife, 1893

DION BOUCICAULT
His First Holiday.
– **Dion Boucicault** suggestion for his tombstone

RICHARD BURBAGE
Exit Burbage. 1619.
– Tombstone inscription

St Leonard's church, Shoreditch, East London

No more young Hamlett, old Heironymoe.
King Leer, the grieved Moore and more beside,
That lived in him, have now for ever dy'de.
– **John Fletcher** attrib. From *An elegie on the death of the famous actor Rich: Burbage*

SAMUEL FOOTE
Foote from his earthly stage, alas! is hurled;
Death took him off, who took off all the world.
– **Samuel Foote** was famous as a mimic; quoted in R. Ryan, *Dramatic Table Talk*, 1825

DAVID GARRICK
I am disappointed by that stroke of death which has eclipsed the gaiety of nations and impoverished the public stock of harmless pleasure.
– **Samuel Johnson** *Epitaph on Garrick*, 1779

WILLIAM S. GILBERT
His foe was folly and his weapon wit.
– **Anthony Hope** inscription

on Gilbert's memorial tablet, Victoria Embankment

OLIVER GOLDSMITH

Here lies Nolly Goldsmith, for
*   shortness called Noll,*
Who wrote like an angel, but
*   talked like poor poll.*
– **David Garrick** 1774

Poet, naturalist, and
    historian,
Who left scarcely any style of
    writing untouched,
And touched none that he
    did not adorn.
– **Samuel Johnson** *Epitaph*
on Goldsmith, 1776

BEN JONSON

O, rare Ben Jonson!
– **John Young** epitaph for
Ben Jonson in Westminster
Abbey. Possibly this should
have read *Orare per* Ben
Jonson ('Pray for Ben
Jonson') but was altered by
the stone-cutter

GEORGE S. KAUFMAN

Over my dead body. – **George
S. Kaufman** when asked to
write his own epitaph

DAN LENO

So little and frail a lantern
could not long harbour so
big a flame.
– **Max Beerbohm** on the
early death, aged 44, of
the popular comic Leno,
who was a mere 5 foot tall.
Obituary, *Saturday Review*,
1904

MARIE LLOYD

Tired she was, and she
*   wouldn't show it.*
Suffering she was, and hoped
*   we didn't know it.*
But He who loved her knew,
*   and, understanding all,*
Prescribed long rest, and gave
*   the final call.*
– Inscription on her
tombstone in Fortune Green
Cemetery

DOROTHY PARKER

Excuse my dust.
– **Dorothy Parker** suggested
epitaph for herself

DOUGLAS QUAYLE

Douglas Quayle Actor
'Resting'
– Gravestone inscription

WILLIAM SHAKESPEARE

Good friends, for Jesus' sake
*   forbear, To dig the dust*
*   enclosed here.*

*Blest be the man that spares
these stones.
And curst be he that moves
my bones.*
– **William Shakespeare**
inscription on his tombstone
at Stratford-upon-Avon

GEORGE BERNARD SHAW
Hic jacet Bernard Shaw.
Who the devil was he?
– suggested epitaph for
himself supplied at the
request of the *London
Evening News*

FAILURE

There is much to be said for
failure. It is more interesting
than success.
– **Max Beerbohm**

There is nothing the British
like more than a bloke who
comes from nowhere, makes
it, and then gets clobbered.
– **Melvyn Bragg** *Rich* (a
biography of Richard
Burton)

*Sing a lament for the plays
that fail –
A dirge for the shows that
fold.*

*A tear on the bier of the flop
of the year
And the tickets that couldn't
be sold.*
– **Howard Dietz** 'Lament for
Failures' from *The Night was
Unruly*

Fifth Column, sixth draft,
seventh producer, eighth
refusal.
– **Ernest Hemingway** on
the disastrous history of his
one and only play; quoted in
M. Zolotow, *No People Like
Show People*, 1951

Even a Hungarian can make
a mistake.
– **Alexander Korda** who
refused a film contract for
Vivien Leigh weeks before
she became a sensation in
The Mask of Virtue, 1936

As a rule, the Flop Obvious,
is caused by a single moment
of delirium, the first point of
deviation from sense, a wild
snatch at flitting fashion.
Managements cannot afford
to be running footmen at
fashion's capricious heels.
– **J. C. Trewin** quoted in D.
Richards, *The Curtain Rises*,
1966

Little except punch drunk optimism can explain an obvious flop. – Ibid.

When you are down and out something always turns up – and it is usually the noses of your friends. – **Oscar Wilde**

FAME

I like to be introduced as America's foremost actor. It saves the necessity of further effort. – **John Barrymore**

None of your Dames for me! I don't want to go about the country labelled and be charged double for everything. – **Lilian Baylis**

A sign of a celebrity is that his name is often worth more than his services.
– **Daniel J. Boorstin**

Once you're a star actor people start asking you questions about politics, astronomy, archaeology and birth control.
– **Marlon Brando**

The despised star system, to true followers of the drama, may appear to be a shameful compromise, but to a hard-working playwright, believe me, it is frequently a very great comfort.
– **Noël Coward**

Theatre people are always pining and agonizing because they're afraid that they'll be forgotten. And in America they're quite right. They will be.
– **Agnes De Mille**

The painter dead, yet still he
* charms the eye,*
While England lives his fame
* can never die.*
But he who struts his hour
* upon the stage*
Can scarce extend his fame
* for half an age.*
No pen nor pencil can the
* actor save;*
The art and artist share one
* common grave.*
– **David Garrick** quoted in Edgar Pemberton, 'The Marvel of Mary Anderson', *Munsey's Magazine*, 1904–5

An actress's life is so transitory – suddenly you're a building.

– **Helen Hayes** 1955, on hearing a New York theatre was to be named after her

Oh, it's great to be a theatre again! – **Helen Hayes** 1983 (The first theatre had been demolished and a new one had been named after her.)

It is the fate of actors to be judged by echoes which are altogether delusive – when they have passed out of immediate ken, and some fifty years hence some old fool will be saying: 'There never was an actor like Irving.'
– **Henry Irving** letter, 1891

It is just as cold in Westminster Abbey as it is in the village churchyard. I don't want to die.
– **Laurence Olivier** interviewed by Gawn Grainger, quoted in A. Holden, *Olivier*, 1988

It is difficult to live up to one's posters . . . when I pass my name in such large letters I blush, but at the same time instinctively raise my hat.

– **Herbert Beerbohm Tree**
Hesketh Pearson, *Beerbohm Tree*, 1956

FANS

Enthusiastic fan to Tallulah Bankhead in mid-performance: I really want to f— you!
Tallulah Bankhead: And so you shall – after the show – you sweet old-fashioned thing. – Attrib.

I lost my nerve in the theatre because of the perfectly sweet fans who came and would break the place up; I hated that, not being in control.
– **Dirk Bogarde** *By Myself*, Channel 4 TV January, 1992

Split me if I'd not a hundred times rather be spoken to by Mr Garrick than His Majesty, God Bless him!
– **Charlotte Burney**

A fan club is a group of people who tell an actor he's not alone in the way he feels about himself.
– **Jack Carson**

Get away, dear! I don't need you any more! – **Norma Talmadge** when approached by a fan a few years after her retirement in 1930

FILM AND TELEVISON

It doesn't matter how 'big' you are as long as you fill it from the inside. – **Alan Badel** 1965; when asked on the set of *Man and Superman* whether a stage performance might seem too 'big' for the television screen; recalled by Martin Jarvis

How often stage and screen, dividing the loyalties of talented actors, have played havoc with their sense of direction and crippled their potentialities in consequence. – **John Gielgud** *Distinguished Company*

A great actor wants to act, which he has more freedom to do on the stage. He doesn't want to worry about mechanical things, as he has to do in the film studios. – **Peter Glenville** 1962

quoted in *Olivier* (ed. L. Gourlay), 1973

I think Charles Laughton did lack technique; when inspiration failed, as fail it often must, he had very little resource either of voice or movement. This often happens when actors, even actors of the greatest talent, whose experience has chiefly been in films, attempt great parts on the stage. – **Tyrone Guthrie** on Laughton's Macbeth at the Old Vic 1934; quoted in *A Life in the Theatre*, 1959

God felt sorry for actors, so he gave them a place in the sun and a swimming-pool; all they had to sacrifice was their talent. – **Cedric Hardwicke** on Hollywood; quoted in S. Morley, *Tales from the Hollywood Raj*, 1983

In the movies you keep everything in. In the theatre you let everything out. **Richard Johnson** *Sunday Times* 28 June 1992

Acting in films is . . . retirement acting – you just

give an exhibition of your former skills.
– **Walter Matthau** 1979, quoted in J. Green, *A Dictionary of Contemporary Quotations*, 1982

Like working in a factory, it was great. You clocked in, said your lines, made sure you didn't fall over the other actors, and hired a van to pick up your wages. Fabulous. – **Ian McShane** on working in the TV soap *Dallas*, quoted in the *Daily Mail*, 28 April 1990

Films are where you sell what you've learned on the stage. – **Ralph Richardson** quoted in A. Holden, *Olivier*, 1988

Don't come too close, you'll see through my talent.
– **Ralph Richardson** attrib. to the lighting cameraman on the set of *The Charge of the Light Brigade*

FINANCE

In merry old England it once was a rule,

The king had his poet and also his fool,
But now we're so frugal, I'd have you to know it,
Poor Cibber must serve both for fool and for poet.
– **Anonymous** on the actor/ dramatist Colley Cibber who was made Poet Laureate in 1730

His cuffs are frayed – offer him £5.00 less.
– **Anonymous producer** after an actor had successfully auditioned for him

I enjoy my little part. As to salary, well, the truth is there isn't much, but there's a real pudding in the second act.
– **Anonymous actor** quoted J. Aye, *Humour in the Theatre*, 1932

There'll be an awful lot of windows to clean.
– **Squire Bancroft** on being shown rival manager Beerbohm Tree's extravagant new theatre, Her Majesty's

It is one of the tragic ironies of the theatre that only one man in it can count

on steady work – the night watchman.
– **Tallulah Bankhead**

Every crowd has a silver lining. – **Phineas T. Barnum**

Dear God, send me a good Hamlet – but make him cheap. – **Lilian Baylis** attrib.

Your excellency, I am accustomed, when I bring an attraction to town, to spend $400 on advertising. As you have done half the advertising for me, I herewith enclose $200 for your parish.
– **Sarah Bernhardt** letter to the Bishop of Chicago who had loudly denounced her 'unsuitable' choice of plays

I can spin out these rough and tumble dramas (*The Poor of New York*) as a hen lays eggs. It's a degrading occupation, but more money has been made out of guano than out of poetry.
– **Dion Boucicault**

To keep up morale in my staff and to fool rival producers and theatrical reporters, I always instructed managers of my road companies to add $300 to their nightly reports of box-office receipts. The system worked fine until one of them wired, 'Only theatre in town burned to ground this afternoon No performance. Receipts $300.'
– **William A. Brady**

When an actor has money he doesn't send letters, but telegrams. – **Anton Chekhov**

I discover that I have not been paid for some time and have decided to withdraw my services. If I'm not paid I don't appear.
– **Albert Finney** quitting *Reflected Glory*, June 1992

Civil servants, treasury officials and cabinet ministers still believe one should work in the arts for honour. – **Peter Hall** *Diaries*, 27 March 1972

With respect to the extravagance of actors, as a traditional character, it is not to be wondered at. They live from hand to mouth:

they plunge from want into luxury; they have no means of making money breed, and all professions that do not live by turning money into money, or have not a certainty of accumulating it in the end by parsimony, spend it. Uncertain of the future, they make sure of the present moment. This is not unwise. **– William Hazlitt** *On Actors and Acting*

I can speak with authority on the subject of being hard up. I have been a provincial actor. **– Jerome K. Jerome** *On the Stage and Off*, 1885

Is it a stale remark to say that I have constantly found the interest excited at a playhouse to bear an exact inverse proportion to the price paid for admission? **– Charles Lamb**

No one ever went broke underestimating the taste of the American Public. **– H. L. Mencken**

Never give a sucker an even break. **– Walter Mizner**

What, ask for a salary when blackberries are ripe! **– John S. Potter** actor-manager, when asked by one of his company for a small part of the money owed him

A guy who likes to wear a black hat and meet blondes. **– Billy Rose** (definition of a theatrical 'angel', who puts up the production money)

Never invest your money in anything that eats or needs repairing. **– Billy Rose**

The trouble with him is that he is in love with his wife and an actor can only afford to be in love with himself. **– George Bernard Shaw**

The trouble, Mr Goldwyn, is that you are only interested in art and I am only interested in money. **– George Bernard Shaw** when Samuel Goldwyn offered to buy the film rights of his plays

I am dying as I have lived – beyond my means. **– Oscar Wilde** on learning the cost of his medical treatment, 1900

Angels with checkbooks rush in where even fools fear to tread. – **Walter Winchell**

FIRST NIGHTS

A first night in London of a Tallulah Bankhead play is a wild orgy of emotion.
– **1920s London theatre critic** quoted in Maurice Zolotow, *No People Like Show People*, 1951

Dear God, please don't let me make a fool of myself tonight.
– **Tallulah Bankhead** ritual prayer before an opening night – followed by a glass of champagne; quoted in Maurice Zolotow, *No People Like Show People*, 1951

I made the usual ritualistic phone calls that I make after a first night. Never mind, never mind, I said.
– **Peter Hall** *Diaries*, 3 May 1974 (after the first night of *Next of Kin* by John Hopkins)

Audience – a gathering of optimists who want to enjoy themselves and hope for the best. Audience, First Night – a gathering of optimists who want to enjoy themselves and hope for the worst.
– **Ronald Jeans** quoted in R. May, *The Wit of the Theatre*, 1969

Opening night is the night before the play is ready to open. – **George Jean Nathan**

A hand on your opening and may your parts grow bigger.
– **Dorothy Parker** first night telegram to Uta Hagen; quoted in R. Huggett, *The Curse of Macbeth*, 1981

I think that first nights should come near the end of a play's run – as indeed they often do. – **Peter Ustinov**

DAVID GARRICK

Garrick was pure gold beat out into thin leaf.
– **James Boswell**

I never saw in my life such brilliant piercing eyes as Mr

Garrick's are. In looking at him, when I have chanced to meet them, I have really not been able to bear their lustre.
– **Fanny Burney** *Diary*, 1771

He contradicted the proverb that one cannot make bricks without straw, by doing what is infinitely more difficult, making actors and actresses without genius.
– **Kitty Clive** *c*.1747

But when . . . I first beheld Garrick, young and light and alive in every muscle and feature, what a transition! It seemed as if a whole century had been stepped over in the transition of a single scene; old things were done away, and a new order at once brought forward, bright and luminous and clearly destined to dispel the barbarism and bigotry of a tasteless age, too long attached to the prejudices of custom, and superstitiously devoted to the illusions of imposing declamation.
– **Richard Cumberland** *Memoirs*, 1806–7

Our Garrick's a salad; for in him we see
Oil, vinegar, sugar and saltness agree.
Though equal to all things, for all things unfit;
Too nice for a statesman, too proud for a wit.
On the stage he was natural, simple, affecting;
'Twas only that when he was off he was acting.
He cast off his friends as a huntsman his pack.
For he knew when he pleas'd he could whistle them back.
Of praise a mere glutton, he swallowed what came,
And the puff of a dunce he mistook it for fame.
– **Oliver Goldsmith** *Retaliation*, 19 April 1774

David, madame, looks much older than he is for his face has had double the business of any other man's: it is never at rest . . . I don't believe he even has the same look for half an hour together in the whole course of his life; and such an eternal, restless, fatiguing play of the muscles must certainly wear out a man's face before its real time.

– **Samuel Johnson** quoted by Fanny Burney, *Diary*, 1778

Garrick, Madam, was no disclaimer; there was not one of his own scene-shifters who could not have spoken 'To be, or not to be' better than he did; yet he was the only actor I ever saw who I could call a master both in comedy and tragedy.
– **Samuel Johnson** to Mrs Siddons; quoted in J. Boswell, *The Life of Samuel Johnson*, 1791

That young man never had his equal and never will have a rival.
– **Alexander Pope**

Garrick . . . made himself a slave to his reputation. ... It was difficult to get him, and when you had him, as difficult to keep him. He never came into company but with a plot how to get out of it.

He was for ever receiving messages of his being wanted in another place. . . . Being used to exhibit himself at a theatre or a large table he did not consider an individual as worth powder and shot.
– **Joshua Reynolds** *Notes on Garrick*

Jack Bannister told me he was behind the scenes one night when Garrick was playing Lear; and that the tones in which Garrick uttered the words 'O fool! I shall go mad!' absolutely thrilled him. – **Samuel Rogers** *Table Talk*, 1856

JOHN GIELGUD

(ON HIMSELF)
What I'd like to do is die on stage in the middle of a good performance and with a full house.

Director **Peter Brook** *was some weeks into rehearsals for* Oedipus *and things were still at the introspective discussion stage, with very little progress on the practical front. As part of the road to self-knowledge each of the cast was asked to think of the most terrifying thing imaginable. When it came to* **Gielgud***'s turn his response was simple*:
We open next Tuesday!

It is a matter of theatrical history that Mr John Gielgud has lost ground during the last three years before the tempestuous onslaught of Mr Laurence Olivier.
– **Beverley Baxter** 1947

Mr Gielgud has the most meaningless legs imaginable.
– **Ivor Brown** reviewing Gielgud as Romeo, May 1924; quoted in D. Rigg, *No Turn Unstoned*, 1982

His tactless remarks, over the decades, have joined the ranks of the happiest theatre legend of our time and, apart from their sheer funniness, they have always been entirely forgivable because they spring spontaneously from the heart, without a glimmer of malice.
– **Alec Guinness** *Blessings in Disguise*, 1985

Sir John Gielgud is the finest actor in the world from the neck up.
– **Kenneth Tynan** 1959

GREEK DRAMA

You know Electra? Well, Electra is like one day in my daughter's life.
– **Sarah Adler** on her actress daughter Celia; quoted in L. Rosenfeld, *Bright Star of Exile*, 1977

Well, that's put the theatre back two and a half thousand years!
– **Noel Davis** on emerging from Peter Hall's acclaimed production of *The Oresteia* 1981

In Aristophanic comedy there was no limit, in word or action, to obscenity. Living men were not only ridiculed, but grossly slandered. Aristophanes seems to have been free to bring any accusations, however monstrous, or cruel, or indecent, against anybody.– **Kenneth Dover** *The Greek World* (ed. H. Lloyd-Jones), 1962

How did the Greeks stand marble benches in their theatres?
– **Aldous Huxley**

The Graces, seeking to possess some sacred enclosure which should never fail, found the soul of Aristophanes.
– **Plato** attrib. inscription for Aristophanes' tomb; quoted by Lord Neaves, *The Greek Anthology*, 1897

IBSEN

These Ibsen creatures are 'neither men nor women, they are ghouls', vile, unlovable, unnatural, morbid monsters and it were well indeed for society if all such went and drowned themselves at once.
– **Review** of the first English production of *Rosmersholm* in *The Gentlewoman*, 1891

A crazy fanatic . . . a crazy cranky being . . . not only consistently dirty but deplorably dull.
– **Review** of Ibsen's *Ghosts,* 1892 (*Ghosts* deals with the subject of venereal disease)

'Peer Gynt' – written by a mad poet. One goes crazy oneself if reading this book.

– **Hans Christian Andersen** 1870

In his bones he is a moralist, in practice an artist.
– **James Huneker**

It was as though someone had dramatized the cooking of a Sunday dinner.
– **Clement Scott** reviewing *The Doll's House* for *Sporting and Dramatic News*, 1889

An open drain, a loathsome sore, an abominable piece, a repulsive and degrading work. – **Clement Scott** review of the first London production of *Ghosts* in the *Daily Telegraph*, 1892

There is no need to enter into the details of so commonplace and suburban a story. In essence it is trivial. – **Clement Scott** reviewing Ibsen's *The Wild Duck* in the *Daily Telegraph* 1894

A reformer who calls you to crawl with him into a sewer, merely to see and breathe its feculence. – **William Winter**

INSULTS

Rachel, French tragedienne, savouring an opening night triumph: 'When I made my entrance the audience sat there completely open-mouthed.' Anonymous fellow actress: 'Nonsense. They never all yawn at exactly the same time.'

If you really want to help the American theatre darling, be an audience.
– **Tallulah Bankhead** to a young actress

Darling, they've absolutely ruined your perfectly dreadful play. – **Tallulah Bankhead** to **Tennessee Williams** after seeing the film of *Orpheus Descending*

The abilities of a young actress were being defended by one of her admirers: 'You must admit she has some wonderful moments.'
Sarah Bernhardt: 'Oh yes, but some terrible half hours.'

It's still the same dear little face we all loved so in Candlelight (pause) – but there's another face round it.
– **Lilian Braithwaite** on French actress **Yvonne Amaud**

The Comtesse de Bremont presents her compliments to Mr W. S. Gilbert and in reply to his answer to her request for an interview for *St. Paul's*, in which he states his terms as twenty guineas for that privilege, begs to say that she anticipates the pleasure of writing his obituary for nothing.
– **Comtesse de Bremont** quoted in G. Snell, *The Book of Theatre Quotes*, 1982

She comes on stage as if she'd been sent for to sew rings on the new curtains.
– **Mrs Patrick Campbell** on **Lillian Gish**

But it's sooo long Mr Jones, even without the Hs.
– **Mrs Patrick Campbell** to **Henry Arthur Jones** who had been reading aloud to her, in his strong cockney accent, his seemingly interminable new play *Michael and His Lost Angel*

Wm. Wheatleigh Esq.,
Manager,
New York City
Dear Sir,
　This will introduce the
eminent tragedian Mr
McKean Buchanen. He
wants to play in New York. I
have seen him play Macbeth,
Richelieu and poker. He
plays the latter best.
– **C. W. Couldock** quoted in
Milton Nobles, *Shop Talk*,
19th century

Who could take that scruffy,
arrogant buffoon seriously?
– **Eddie Fisher** on Richard
Burton (who had taken
Fisher's wife, Elizabeth
Taylor)

Tallulah Bankhead to Lynn
Fontanne: How lucky you
are to be married to Alfred
Lunt, darling. His directing,
his acting, his theatre sense.
Where would you be without
it?'
Lynn Fontanne: 'Probably
playing your parts.'

Oh to be in England now
that June's here.
– **Judy Garland** on the
Broadway debut of English

actress Lady June Inverclyde

I only have a misleading
lady. – **W. S. Gilbert** on
a disappointing piece of
casting quoted in J. Aye,
Humour in the Theatre, 1932

You – effeminate guys of the
theatre, what do you know
about real war!
– **Ernest Hemingway**

She knows when she should
come on, and she knows
when she should go off – it's
the bit in the middle that
foxes her.
– **Hugh Hunt** on an
unnamed actress

She has made an acting style
out of post-nasal drip.
– **Pauline Kael** on **Sandy
Dennis**

Tallulah who?
– **Beatrice Lillie**

Pauline Kael has aptly
observed that Miss Dennis
'has made an acting style out
of post-nasal drip'. It should
be added that she balanced
her post-nasal condition
with something like a pre-

frontal lobotomy, so that when she is not a walking catarrh she is a blithering imbecile. – **John Simon** reviewing *The Fox*, 1968

Diana Rigg is built like a brick mausoleum with insufficient flying buttresses. – **John Simon** 1970 (Miss Rigg had appeared naked in *Abelard and Heloise*)

Ah . . . (pause). Your father was a great actor. – **Constantin Stanislavski** to Joseph Schildkraut after seeing him in Peer Gynt, 1923. Schildkraut's father was the renowned Viennese actor Rudolf Schildkraut.

Among the select group of plays written for eminent husband and wife teams in coronation years, it ranks very high. ·· **Kenneth Tynan** 1953, on Terence Rattigan's *The Sleeping Prince*, written for Laurence Olivier and Vivien Leigh

Miss Ilona Massey, the blonde film actress who is making her Broadway debut in this production is doubtless very good in films. – **Willela Waldorf** *New York Post*

If I can't go to their openings I'll wait three days and go to their closings. – **Walter Winchell** *c.*1920; on the Shubert brothers, who had banned the critic from their theatres

Alexander Woollcott to Peggy Wood: I don't think you would make a good Lady Macbeth. Do you? **Peggy Wood** to Alexander Woollcott: No. but you would.

HENRY IRVING

(ON HIMSELF)
For an actor who can't walk, can't talk and has no face to speak of, I've done pretty well. – **Henry Irving** to Ellen Terry

(BY OTHERS)
He danced, he did not merely walk – he sang, he by no means merely spoke. He was essentially artificial, in

distinction to being merely natural.
– **Edward Gordon Craig**
Henry Irving, 1931

I go to the pantomime only at Christmas.
– **W. S. Gilbert** when asked if he had seen Irving as Faust

Of what the French call diction – of the art of delivery – he has apparently not a suspicion. This forms three fourths of an actor's obligations and in Mr Irving's acting these three fourths are simply cancelled.
– **Henry James** *Scenic Art*

He achieved the celebrated feat of performing Hamlet with the part of Hamlet omitted and all other parts as well, substituting for it and for them the fascinating figure of Henry Irving, which for many years did not pall on his audience and never palled on himself.
– **George Bernard Shaw** preface to *Ellen Terry and Bernard Shaw* (ed. C. St. John), 1931

He does not merely cut plays; he disembowels them.
– **George Bernard Shaw** 'Blaming the Bard', *Saturday Review*, September 1896

He has an ugly ear! Large, flabby, ill-cut, and pasty looking, pale and lumpy.
– **Ellen Terry** *Notes on Irving*

The hero, though a mannerist of the Macready type, acted wonderfully . . . The way in which Irving acted his own dream, and describes the way in which he carried out the murder, is wonderful and ghastly, as well as the scene at his death . . . it was a most successful performance.
– **Queen Victoria** on Irving's command performance of *The Bells* at Windsor Castle, 1889

I am very, very pleased.
– **Queen Victoria** to Irving when she dubbed him the first ever theatrical Knight in 1895

Irving's legs are distinctly precious, but his left leg is a poem.
– **Oscar Wilde**

EDMUND KEAN

(ON HIMSELF)

Fight for me, I have no resources in myself; mind is gone and the body is hopeless. God knows my heart. I would do but cannot. Memory, the first of goddesses, has forsaken me, and I am left without a hope but from those old resources that the public and myself are tired of. Damn God, damn ambition. The soul leaps, the body falls.
– Letter to W. H. Halpin, 1830; quoted in Peter Hall, *Diaries*, 1982

(BY OTHERS)

With . . . Byron to a private pit box to see Mr Kean in Richard III. He was extremely happy: and is a very short man with a piercing black eye. 'Off with his head; so much for Buckingham', was given thus; The instant he received the news of Buckingham being prisoner he said quickly, 'Off with his head', and then, advancing to the front of the stage, added with a savage smile, 'So much for Buckingham.'
– **Lord Broughton** *Recollections of a Long Life*, 1865

Kean is original; but he copies from himself.
– **Samuel Taylor Coleridge** 27 April 1823; quoted in *Table Talk and Omniana* (ed. T. Ashe), 1884

To see him act is like reading Shakespeare by flashes of lightning. – Ibid.

There is in Mr Kean an infinite variety of talent, with a certain monotony of genius.
– **William Hazlitt** 'Mr Kean's Duke Aranza', *The Examiner*, 10 December 1815

You cannot say that Kean has style. You can only judge his performance by the number of electrical shocks in it. – **William Hazlitt**

If he was irregular and unartistlike in his performance so is Niagara compared with the waterworks of Versailles.
– **Fanny Kemble** quoted in

M. Billington, *The Guinness Book of Theatre Facts and Feats*, 1982

No Sir, I did not see Mr Kean. I saw Othello; and further, I shall not act the part again.
– **John Philip Kemble** on being asked by a friend if he had seen the 'little man Kean' on stage the night before

I went to see Mr Kean and was thoroughly disgusted. This monarch of the stage is a little, insignificant man, slightly deformed, strongly ungraceful, seldom pleasing to the eye, still seldomer satisfying to the ear – with a voice between grunting and croaking, a perpetual hoarseness which suffocates his words and a vulgarity of manner which his admirers are pleased to call mature.
– **Mary Russell Mitford** Letter, 3 July 1814

Kean! Ah Kean! I saw him once. He was a splendid Gipsy.
– **Arthur Wing Pinero** *Trelawney of the Wells*, 1898

Edmund Kean, the great flamboyant 19th-century actor, is said to have varied his diet according to the part he had to play. For tyrants he would eat roast pork. For murderers, raw beef. For lovers, boiled mutton. There is no record of the roles he played when he ate ham.
– **Dick Richards** *The Curtain Rises*, 1966

KITCHEN SINK

What does he show? Lentils boiling in a pot while six men march up and down. Is this entertainment?
– **Noël Coward** attrib. on the plays of Arnold Wesker

Since the war a terrible pall of significance has fallen over plays.
– **Noël Coward** to James Dow on the theatre of the 1950s; quoted in D. Richards, *The Wit of Noël Coward*

Contemporary English drama is the measuring out of life in tepid teacups.
– *The Times*, 1965

VIVIEN LEIGH

By Jove, she's a clinker!
– **Winston Churchill**

She was often underrated
because she was so beautiful.
– **George Cukor** quoted in
Gavin Lambert, *On Cukor*

Everyone talks about the
lovely place Vivien had in
London. Well, it always
smelled like kitty litter,
which she kept in the hall.
– **Joan Fontaine** quoted in
Celebrity Gossip

She made life hell for
everyone near her, unless
they did everything she
wished, as she wished and
when she wished.
– **Wolfe Kaufman**

I only saw Vivien Leigh
once in my life in person.
That was at the Ritz-Carlton
Hotel in Boston. I got into
the elevator and she was
there. And I got goose
pimples. I got off on the
third floor, like a fool. The
goose pimples remained
for ten minutes which,
I am told, is a medical

phenomenon.
– **Walter Matthau**

She had big hands and
packed a hefty slap.
– **Alec McCowen** (who was
slapped nightly by Miss
Leigh in the 1952 *Antony and
Cleopatra*), *Sunday Times*,
19 January 1992

She wanted us to be like
brother and sister. But,
fortunately, occasional incest
was allowed.
– **Laurence Olivier**

You are the Mrs Pat
Campbell of the age.
– **George Bernard Shaw** 1942

She had the misfortune to be
one of the most physically
beautiful actresses of her
period.
– **J. C. Trewin** quoted in
Vivien Leigh's obituary in
the *Observer*, 1967

She picks at the part with
the daintiness of a debutante
called upon to dismember
a stag.
– **Kenneth Tynan** on
Vivien Leigh in *Antony and
Cleopatra*, 1951

When she takes the stage she commands it as if she had first arrived there suspended from the bill of a stork.
– **Tennessee Williams**
quoted in A. Walker, *Vivien*, 1987

OSCAR LEVANT

(ON HIMSELF)
I'm a controversial figure: my friends either dislike me or hate me. – Quoted by Walter Winchell in *Winchell Exclusive*, 1975

(BY OTHERS)
Oscar was a man of principle. He never sponged off anybody he didn't admire. – **Harpo Marx**

When Oscar comes on stage he weaves on like a drunk trying to find the rest room.
– **Jack Paar**

Oscar has mellowed – like an old pistol. – **Billy Rose**

There's nothing wrong with Oscar Levant – nothing that a miracle couldn't fix.
– **Alexander Woollcott**

To autograph seekers he has only three words: 'Go to Hell'. – **Maurice Zolotov**

LIFE

A quarrel in the theatrical world usually ends in one actor taking another's part.
– **John Aye** *Humour in the Theatre*, 1932

But men must know, that in this theatre of man's life it is reserved only for Gods and angels to be lookers-on.
– **Francis Bacon** *The Advancement of Learning*, Bk. II, Ch. 20

Life – with a capital F!
– **Lilian Baylis**

Life begets life. Energy creates energy. It is by spending oneself that one becomes rich.
– **Sarah Bernhardt**

To others we are not ourselves but a performer in their lives cast for a part we do not even know we are playing. – **Elizabeth Bibesco** *Haven*, 1951

An actress without talent, forty years old, ate a partridge for dinner, and I felt sorry for the partridge, for it occurred to me that in its life it had been more talented, more sensible, and more honest than the actress. – **Anton Chekhov** *Notebooks*, 1892–94

The trouble with Freud is that he never played the Glasgow Empire Saturday night. – **Ken Dodd** *The Times*, 1965; quoted in J. Green, *A Dictionary of Contemporary Quotations*, 1982

For, Heaven be thanked, we
    live in such an age,
When no man dies for love,
    but on the stage.
– **Mithridates**

Everybody has his own theatre, in which he is manager, actor, prompter, playwright, scene- shifter, boxkeeper, doorkeeper, all in one, and audience into the bargain.
– **Julius and Augustus Hare** *Guesses at Truth*, 1827

Life used to be full of third acts, bringing everything nicely to a comforting close, with a satisfying solution. But life isn't like that any longer. There is no solution. You can't send people back to their homes any more with their problems solved. If you did solve their problems, they just wouldn't believe it.
– **Laurence Olivier** quoted in A. Holden, *Olivier*, 1988

All the world's a stage,
And all the men and women
    merely players:
They have their exits and
    their entrances;
And one man in his time
    plays many parts,
His acts being seven ages.
– **William Shakespeare**
As You Like It, Act II, Scene 7

When we are born we cry that
    we are come
To this great stage of fools.
– **William Shakespeare**
King Lear, Act IV, Scene 6

Life's but a walking shadow, a
    poor player,
That struts and frets his hour
    upon the stage,

And then is heard no more.
– **William Shakespeare**
Macbeth, Act V, Scene 5

I hold the world but as the
world, Gratiano;
A stage, where every man
must play a part,
And mine a sad one.
– **William Shakespeare** *The*
Merchant of Venice, Act 1,
Scene 1

THE LUNTS

(ON THEMSELVES)
We can be bought but we
can't be bored.
– **Alfred Lunt and Lynn**
Fontanne quoted in Alfred
Lunt's obituary, 1977

(BY OTHERS)
They are deeply concerned
with only three things –
themselves, the theatre
(in so far as it concerns
themselves), and food –
good, hot food.
– **Noël Coward** *Diaries*,
17 September 1953

Alfred Lunt has his head in
the clouds and his feet in the
box office. – **Noël Coward**

If you want a play to run
    many a munt,
Get Lynn Fontanne and
    Alfred Lunt.
– **Robert Sherwood** quoted
in S. N. Behrman, *People in a*
Diary, 1972

Their attitude can most
clearly be expressed by a
child's copybook maxim,
about duty; doing their
duty towards the play, the
dramatist, the audience,
according to their own high
standards. – **G. B. Stern**

MELODRAMA

Listen to me, Your Lordship.
You have broken up my
business, you have ruined
my home, you have sent my
son to prison and my wife
to a dishonoured grave, and
you have seduced my only
daughter. But, have a care,
Lord Fitz Wallop, I am a
man of quick temper. Do not
try me too far.
– **Horace Wyndham**
melodrama epitomized;
quoted in J. Aye, *Humour in*
the Theatre, 1932

METHOD ACTING

A man of the theatre died last night: – It will take a hundred years before the harm that man has done to the art of acting can be corrected. – **Stella Adler** on learning of the death of **Lee Strasberg**, 1982

I should like you to convey when you are acting it that the man you portray has a brother in Shropshire who drinks port.
– **J. M. Barrie** to an anxious actor seeking help in interpreting his part

He had two rules for playing with Method actors: 1. Let them improvise to their hearts' content and just wait for your cue; and 2. Don't ever play an eating scene with them, because they spit all over you.
– **Humphrey Bogart** recalled by Nathaniel Benchley in *Celebrity Gossip*, 1984

Mr Strasberg went off into a long dissertation on the art of acting, most of which was pretentious balls.
– **Noël Coward** *Diaries*, 25 May 1958

If you must have motivation think of your pay packet on Friday.
– **Noël Coward** 1926; quoted in Sheridan Morley, *A Talent to Amuse*, 1985

Well I have a bash at it, and if it doesn't go, I have another bash at it.
– **Wendy Hiller** when asked about her 'method' by an American reporter; quoted in P. Hay, *Broadway Anecdotes*, 1989

I don't want any of that Stanislavski shit from you.
– **Charles Laughton** to Eli Wallach before rehearsals for *Major Barbara*; quoted in D. Garfield, *The Actor's Studio*, 1980

It is a simple common sense approach to releasing and bringing in to play the creative powers that all actors have in them by virtue of themselves being living human beings.
– **Clifford Odets** quoted in *Acting – A Handbook of the*

Stanislavski Method (ed. T. Cole), 1947

It teaches not how to play this or that part but how to create organically.
– **Lee Strasberg** quoted in *Acting – A Handbook of the Stanislavski Method*

The connection between role and soul. – **Lee Strasberg**

The Method as practised by the *New York Actors' Studio* under Lee Strasberg not only sank the actor into his part, it completely lost him. And that is the basic difference between Stanislavski and The Method.
– **Michael R. Turner** *Bluff Your Way in the Theatre*, 1967

MOTIVATION

The whole motivation for any performer: 'Look at me, Ma!' – **Lenny Bruce**

I've done the most awful rubbish in order to have somewhere to go in the morning.
– **Richard Burton**

Actors are like racehorses. You just rein them in or whip them on and make sure you give them a lump of sugar if they do well.
– **Terry Hands** quoted in M. Billington, *The Guinness Book of Theatre Facts and Feats*, 1982

Now that we have a surplus female population it is clear that all women cannot marry, they cannot enlist, nor yet go out to the colonies and become domestic servants. So they sigh after the stage.
– **George Moore** 1886

The more intelligent of my young colleagues, in ceaseless talks seeking some rationalization of our lives, agree that their choice of metier was to satisfy an urgent need to express themselves . . . I have to confess, rather shamefacedly, that I have never been conscious of any need other than to show off.
– **Laurence Olivier** *Confessions of an Actor*, 1982

All the inspiration I ever needed was a telephone call from a producer.
– **Cole Porter**

You don't act to earn your living. You act to lie, to lie to yourself, to be what you cannot be and because you're fed up with what you are. You act so as not to know yourself, and because you know yourself too well. You act because you're a liar from birth. You act because you'd go mad if you didn't.
– **Jean-Paul Sartre** *Kean*, 1954 (translated by Frank Hauser)

MUSIC HALL/ VAUDEVILLE

She had a heart as big as Waterloo station.
– **James Agate** about music-hall star **Marie Lloyd**

The aim of the music-hall is, in fact, to cheer the lower classes up by showing them a life uglier and more sordid than their own.
– **Max Beerbohm**

With the collapse of vaudeville new talent has no place to sink.
– **George Burns**

Vaudeville is a species of entertainment derived from the dregs of drama and musical comedy, assembled in such wise that they shall appeal to the dregs of the drama and musical comedy audiences.
– **George Jean Nathan** *American Mercury*, 1929

The domestic back parlour of music-hall itself.
– **John Osborne** on theatrical digs in *A Better Class of Person*, 1981

Every performance given by Marie Lloyd is a Command Performance by order of the British Public.
– Poster for **Marie Lloyd**'s performance at the Pavilion Theatre, 1912. She had been left out of the Royal Command performance on the same night because her three marriages and two divorces were considered too scandalous for George V and Queen Mary.

MUSICALS

Facts and Feats, 1982

I must say Bernard Shaw is greatly improved by music.
– **T. S. Eliot** on *My Fair Lady*, 1958

The trouble with nude dancing is that not everything stops when the music stops.
– **Robert Helpmann** after seeing *Oh! Calcutta*, 1969

Musicals – a series of catastrophes ending with a floor show. – **Oscar Levant**

An American musical so bad that at times I longed for the boy-meets-tractor theme of Soviet drama. – **Bernard Levin** on *Flower Drum Song* in the *Daily Express*, 1960

Definition of a musical – disorderly conduct occasionally interrupted by talk. – **L. L. Levinson**

These shows are to the theatres what wines are to a substantial dinner.
– **George Jean Nathan** quoted in M. Billington, *The Guinness Book of Theatre*

It seems that the moment anyone gets hold of an exclamation mark these days, he promptly writes a musical show around it.
– **George Jean Nathan**

There will be a quick rash of hairy American filth, but it shouldn't threaten the existence of decent, serious British filth.
– **John Osborne** writing in *Time* magazine after the London opening of the American musical *Hair*

As synthetic and padded as the transvestite's cleavage.
– **Frank Rich** on *La Cage aux Folles* in the *New York Times*, 1983

I had to hit myself on the head afterwards with a small hammer to get that stupid *Tomorrow* song out of my head. – **Ian Shoales** on *Annie*, 1977

Musicals – millions of pounds riding on a piece of piffle. – **Mark Steyn** Channel 4 TV, 10 March 1992

LAURENCE OLIVIER

I believe I was born to be an actor. – *Sunday Times*, 3 November 1963

An actor is a sitting duck in any case, but an actor who is a Lord is a duck flying straight towards you, a figure of fun. – After becoming the first actor to receive a peerage, 1970

I am an actor because that is all I am qualified to do. I shall go on acting until a couple more illnesses cause me to drop. And then I shall write that dreaded book. – *Los Angeles Times*, 26 February 1978

I am far from sure when I am acting and when I am not. Or, more frankly, when I am lying and when I am not. For what is good acting but convincing lying? – *Confessions of an Actor*, 1982

I may be rather feminine but I am not effeminate. – Quoted by M. Billington

in *Olivier: In Celebration* (ed. G. O'Connor), 1988

I don't enjoy acting, but I can't live without it. I'm like a sort of carthorse with a collar round its neck: if you take it off, it starts whinnying for it. – Quoted in A. Holden, *Olivier*, 1988

A comedian by instinct and a tragedian by art. – **James Agate** quoted in A. Walker, *Vivien*, 1987

No actor before him has ever triumphed in such a wide diversity of roles or created so much history. – **Michael Billington** *The Guinness Book of Theatre Facts and Feats*, 1982

Gulping down his lines as if they were so many bad oysters. – **John Mason Brown** reviewing the New York production of *Romeo and Juliet* in the *Post*, 1940

This Oedipus is one of those performances in which

blood and electricity are somehow mixed. It pulls down lightning from the sky. It is as awesome, dwarfing and appalling as one of nature's angriest displays.
– **John Mason Brown** on *Oedipus Rex*, New York 1946 in *Seeing Things* 1946

He came on smelling a rose, laughing softly with a private delight; barefooted, ankleted, black.
– **Ronald Bryden** on Olivier's *Othello* at the Old Vic, 1964

Olivier brandished his technique like a kind of stylistic alibi. In catching the eye he frequently disengaged the brain. – **Russell Davies** Channel 4 TV, 3 March 1992

Olivier is a great impersonator. I am always myself.
– **John Gielgud** quoted in A. Holden *Olivier*, 1988

He handicapped himself by wearing a beard and mane so stupendous that his voice came to me as though he were talking through a tree.
– **Hubert Griffith** *Sunday*

Graphic review of Olivier's King Lear, 1946

Offstage he was not notably handsome or striking, but with make-up he could achieve a flashing Italianate, rather saturnine, but fascinating appearance. The voice already had a marvellous ringing baritone brilliance at the top; he spoke with a beautiful and aristocratic accent, with keen intelligence and a strong sense of rhythm. He moved with catlike agility. He had, if anything, too strong an instinct for the sort of theatrical effect which is striking and memorable. From the first moment of the first rehearsal it was evident that here was no ordinary actor, not everyone's cup of tea – no very strong personality can be that; not necessarily well-cast for Hamlet, but inevitably destined for the very top of the tree.
– **Tyrone Guthrie** 1937; *A Life in the Theatre*, 1959

Acting is not imitation but revelation of the inner self.

This is not what Larry does or sets out to do. He is a performer.
– **Peter Hall** quoted in A. Holden, *Olivier* ,1988

The theatre is his form of Church – a temple to man's knowledge of man, a place where people gather together and somebody talks to them and they are moved.
– **Joan Plowright** (wife) quoted in A. Holden, *Olivier*, 1988

The very boldness of Larry's personality, his natural drive and his pragmatism make him unsuitable to play an introspective, wavering character like Hamlet.
– **Michael Redgrave** *In My Mind's Eye*, 1983

He will spend 30 seconds sizing you up, decide what kind of person you want him to be, and then he will turn into that person.
– **Kenneth Tynan**

He is our model Richard III and his Hotspur is unique, but he has no intrinsic majesty; he always fights shy of pathos; and he cannot play old men without letting his jaw sag and his eyes wander archly in magpie fashion – in short, without becoming funny.
– **Kenneth Tynan** after seeing Olivier's Lear, 1946

I had been told this was the last flourish of romantic acting. It's nothing of the sort. It's an anthology of everything that has been discovered about acting in the last three centuries.
– **Franco Zeffirelli** on Olivier's Othello, 1964, in K. Tynan, *The Sound of Two Hands Clapping*, 1975

OPPROBRIUM

Stage plays are the most petulant, the most impure, impudent, wicked, unclean, the most shameful and detestable atonements of filthy devil-gods.
– **St Augustine of Hippo**

The Theatres – those Cages of Uncleanness, and public schools of Debauchery.
– **St Augustine of Hippo**

What need I comment on the lewdness of those spectacles, and give a detailed description? For what is to be met with there but lewd laughing, and smut, ranting and buffoonery? In a word it is all Scandal and Confusion.
– **St John Chrysostom**

Spending time in theatres, produces fornication, intemperance, and every kind of impurity.
– **St John Chrysostom**

He diverts the ladies with the charming rhetoric of *snotty-nose*, *filthy vermin in the beard*, *nitty jerkin*, *louse-snapper*, and *letter in the chamber pot;* and with an abusive description of a countess, and a rude story of a certain lady with some other varieties of this kind too coarse to mention. . . . There is more physic than comedy in such sentences as these. *Crocus metallorum* will scarce turn the stomach more effectively.
– **Jeremy Collier** *A Short View of the Immorality and Profaneness of the English Stage*, 1698. Collier was commenting on Thomas D'Urfey's *Don Quixote* which typified the lewdness of the period.

I am persuaded that Satan hath not a more speedy way and fitter school to work and teach his desire, to bring men and women into his share of concupiscence and filthy lusts of wicked whoredom, than those plays and theatres. – **John Northbrooke** *Spiritus est Vicarius Christi in Terra*, 1579

Stage plays . . . are sinfull, heathenish, lewde, ungodly Spectacles, and most pernicious Corruptions, condemned in all ages, as intolerable Mischiefs to Churches, to Republickes, to the manners, mindes and soules of men. And . . . the profession of Play-poets, of Stage-players; together with the penning, acting, and frequenting of Stage-playes, are unlawful, infamous and misbeseeming Christians.
– **William Prynne** *Histrio-Mastix: The Players Scourge or Actors Tragedie*, 1633

Do they [plays] not maintain bawdry, insinuate foolery, and renew the remembrance of heathen idolatry? Do they not induce whoredom and uncleanness? Nay, are they not rather plain devourers of maidenly virginity and chastity? – **Philip Stubbes** *Anatomie of Abuses*, 1583

There is a total extinction of all taste; our authors are vulgar, illiberal: the theatre swarms with wretched translations, and ballad operas, and we have nothing new but improving abuse.
– **Horace Walpole**

l understand they [plays] are now forbidden because of the plague. I like the policy well if it hold still, for a disease is but lodged or patched up that is not cured in the cause, and the cause of plagues is sin, if you look to it well; and the causes of sin are plays; therefore the cause of plagues are plays.
– **Thomas White**

Nudity on stage? I think it's disgusting. But if I were 22 with a great body, it would be artistic, tasteful, patriotic and a progressive religious experience.
– **Shelley Winters**

PANTOMIME

The smell of wee-wee and oranges.
– **Tommy Trinder** definition of pantomime

PLAYS

Aristotle
Took another swig from the bottle,
And remarked to a friend:
'A play must have a beginning,
A middle and an end.'
– **Anon.**, quoted in G. Snell, *The Book of Theatre Quotes*, 1982

Very few plays are any good and no first plays are any good.
– **George Abbot** *Saturday Evening Post*, 1955

The greater the play the less production it will need.
– **James Agate**

I don't see why people need new plays all the time. What would happen to concerts if people wanted new music all the time? – **Clive Barnes**

Plays are not written, they are rewritten.
– **Dion Boucicault** a playwright, famous for his 'adaptations'

A play is like a cigar. If it is a failure, no amount of puffing will make it draw. If it is a success everybody wants a box. – **Henry J. Byron**

If a gun is hanging on the wall in the first act it must fire in the last.
– **Anton Chekhov**

The most important ingredients of a play are life, death, food, sex and money, but not necessarily in that order. – **Noël Coward**

If the critics unanimously take exception to one particular scene it is advisable to move that scene to a more conspicuous place in the programme.
– **Noël Coward**

When they told me the day of the well-made play was over, all I could think was, thank God the day of the well-made aeroplane isn't over. – **Noël Coward** quoted in R. May, *The Wit of the Theatre*, 1969

The stage play is a trial, not a deed of violence. The soul is opened, like the combination of a safe, by means of a word. You don't require an acetylene torch.
– **Jean Giraudoux**

I believe that the theatre begins with the word. In the beginning there is the word. Absolutely! – **Peter Hall**

One begins with two people on a stage and one of them had better say something pretty damn quick.
– **Moss Hart** *Contemporary Dramatists*, 1977

I believe that plays that are successful are usually more entertaining than plays that fail. This will come as a revolutionary idea only to those who allow themselves to be intimidated by small critics who work for small quarterlies. – **Jean Kerr** quoted in D. Richards, *The Curtain Rises*, 1966

Good dialogue is like the most charming interior of a house, but it is of little use if the foundations are insecure and the drains don't work. – **Somerset Maugham** to **Noël Coward**, quoted in M. Billington, *The Guinness Book of Theatre Facts and Feats*, 1982

The most exciting form of writing is the writing of plays. – **A. A. Milne** *It's Too Late Now*, 1939

The only rule I have found to have any meaning in writing is to try and not bore yourself. – **John Mortimer** *Five Plays* (Introduction), 1971

Much of the contemporary English polite comedy writing suggests a highly polished and very smooth billiard table with all the necessary brightly polished cues but without balls.
– **George Jean Nathan**

Encyclopaedia of the Theatre, 1940

American playwriting by and large enjoys all the attributes of a violin, save only its melodiousness. The necessary guts are there, but the bow lacks the gift of evoking poetic song from them. – Ibid.

Five surefire indications the play will be terrible:
 When, as the curtain goes up, you hear the newsboys shouting, 'Extra! Extra!"
 As soon as you hear the line, 'If a man kills a man, that's murder. Why isn't it then also murder if a man in uniform does the same thing? War is murder!'
 Any mystery in which, at the very start, someone remarks that the nearest house is two miles away.
 The moment anyone puts something into a drawer with a furtive look.
 Any translation from the Hungarian in which the heroine is called Countess Katinka. – Ibid.

We English are more violent

than we allow ourselves to know. That is why we have the greatest body of dramatic literature in the world. – **John Osborne**

My own view is that a play that is susceptible to crucial rewriting in rehearsal should never have reached that stage. – **John Osborne** *Almost a Gentleman*, 1991

The play's the thing
Wherein I'll catch the
    conscience of the king.
– **William Shakespeare**
Hamlet, Act II, Scene 2

Is there no play,
To ease the anguish of a
    torturing hour?
– **William Shakespeare**
A Midsummer Night's
Dream, Act V, Scene 1

There must be something radically wrong with a play if it pleases everybody.
– **George Bernard Shaw** 1914; after the success of *Pygmalion*

Through all the drama –
    whether damn'd or not –
Love gilds the scene, and
women guide the plot.
– **Richard Brinsley Sheridan**
The Rivals, 1775

It is a received point among poets, that where history gives you a good heroic outline for a play, you may fill up with a little love at your own discretion. (Mr Puff) – **Richard Brinsley Sheridan** *The Critic*, 1779

Ever while you live have two plots to your tragedy. The grand point in managing them is only to let your underplot have as little connexion with your main plot as possible. (Mr Puff) – Ibid.

A good many inconveniences attend playgoing in any large city, but the greatest of them all is usually the play itself.
– **Kenneth Tynan** *New York Herald Tribune*, 1957

There can be no great drama without a noble national life, and the commercial spirit of England has killed that.
– **Oscar Wilde** *The English Renaissance of Art* (lecture), 1882

PLAYWRIGHTS

There are no dull subjects,
only dull playwrights.
– **Robert Anderson**

Dramatist – one who adapts
plays from the French.
– **Ambrose Bierce** *The
Devil's Dictionary*

I always think the poor
playwright is the most
scurvily-treated being in the
theatre. – **Denys Blakelock**
Advice to a Player, 1958

You've got to love the real
world if you're a dramatist,
and if the real world is not as
you like it, then that's got to
be the stuff of your drama,
or you end up with windy,
hollow, romantic writing.
– **Howard Brenton** *The
Times*, 13 April 1992

Our poets make us laugh
at Tragedy. And with their
Comedies they make us cry.
– **George Villiers, 2nd Duke
of Buckingham**

Poor man. He's completely
unspoiled by failure.
– **Noël Coward** attrib. on

a successful but over-rated
playwright

Wise beginners of
playwrights will, of course,
after a little while compare
their press notices with their
royalties and decide that
they still have a great deal to
learn. – **Noël Coward**

What is there in your play
that is so deep? Apart from
the plot, which is completely
submerged after the first
four pages. – **Noël Coward**

Any dramatist finds that his
plays fall into two categories:
those for which he had some
hopes but which went wrong
either in the writing or in
the production; and those
for which he had none, and
which surprised him by
achieving public approval.
– **Ronald Duncan** *Collected
Plays*, 1971

Conflict is the force that
drives a theatrical writer.
– **Dario Fo** *The Independent*,
1 April 1992

We have given a comedy of
M. Viennet in order not to

be obliged to play one of his tragedies. – **Arsene Houssaye** *Behind the Scenes at the Comédie Française*, 1889

I think paradise will be regained on 44th Street when young playwrights understand that they must try not to write plays that will cause nice ordinary people from Riverdale to wish they were dead. – **Jean Kerr** quoted in D. Richards, *The Curtain Rises*, 1966

There are three primal urges in human beings: food, sex, and rewriting someone else's play.– **Romulus Linney** quoted in P. Hay, *Theatrical Anecdotes*, 1987

The only truth which is demanded from the dramatist is truth to character. Subject to this truth he is required to present in the refracting mirror of the stage such distortion of real life as will best reflect his meaning. – **A. A. Milne** *It's Too Late Now*, 1939

I've left a trail of richer but sadder authors after me. – **Robert Morley** quoted in his obituary, *The Times*, 4 June 1992

An actor without a playwright is like a hole without a doughnut. – **George Jean Nathan** quoted in M. Billington, *The Guinness Book of Theatrical Facts and Feats*, 1982

Agents and managers like their popular models to be annually unchanged. If the new Ayckbourn or Stoppard is too unlike the last one there will be complaints from those who had got such reliable mileage from previous makes. – **John Osborne** *A Better Class of Person*, 1981

Most playwrights should observe the same constitutional rights as the Queen: to be consulted, to advise and to warn. – **John Osborne** *Almost a Gentleman*, 1991

If you can't write a play without being taught – don't. – **George Bernard Shaw**

Writing a play is like smashing that [glass] ashtray, filming it in slow motion, and then running the film in reverse, so that the fragments of rubble seem to fly together. You start – or at least I start – with the rubble.
– **Tom Stoppard** quoted in K. Tynan, *Show People*, 1980

A playwright is a lay preacher peddling the ideas of his time in popular form.
– **August Strindberg**

My Dear Sir,
I have read your play. Oh, my dear Sir!
Yours faithfully etc.
– **Herbert Beerbohm Tree** reply to an aspiring playwright

Show me a congenital eavesdropper with the instincts of a Peeping Tom and I will show you the makings of a dramatist.
– **Kenneth Tynan** *Pausing on the Stairs*, 1957

The first rule for a young playwright to follow is not to write like Henry Arthur Jones . . . The second and third rules are the same.
– **Oscar Wilde**

An incinerator is a writer's best friend.
– **Thornton Wilder** *New York Times*, 6 November 1961

PLAYWRIGHTS
– Individuals

SAMUEL BECKETT
It was an expression, symbolic in order to avoid all personal error, by an author who expected each member of his audience to draw his own conclusions, make his own errors. It asked nothing in point, it forced no dramatized moral on the viewer, it held out no specific hope. . . . We're still waiting for Godot, and shall continue to wait. When the scenery gets too drab and the action too slow, we'll call each other names and swear to part forever – but then, there's no place to go.
– Review of a production of *Waiting for Godot* in San Quentin prison, *San Quentin News*, 28 November 1957;

quoted in M. Esslin, *The Theatre of the Absurd*, 1962

You either like Samuel Beckett's plays or you think they are a heap of twaddle. They remind me of something John Betjeman might do if you filled him up with Benzedrine and then force fed him intravenously with Guinness.
– **Tom Davies** *Observer*, 17 June 1979; quoted in F. S. Pepper, *The Dictionary of Biographical Quotations*, 1985

Beckett's *Waiting for Godot* . . . arrived in London ten years ago like a sword burying itself in an over-upholstered sofa.
– **Penelope Gilliatt** review in the *Observer* quoted in M. Billington, *The Guinness Book of Theatre Facts and Feats*, 1982

A play in which nothing happens twice.
– **Vivian Mercier** on *Waiting for Godot* quoted in G. Snell, *The Book of Theatre Quotes*, 1982

I suspect that Beckett is a confidence trick perpetrated on the twentieth century by a theatre-hating God. He remains the only playwright in my experience capable of making forty minutes seem like an eternity and the wrong kind of eternity at that. – **Sheridan Morley** *Punch*, 1973

The suggestion that something is being said about the human predicament won't hold water any more than Beckett's incontinent heroes can. – *Spectator* 1959; quoted in C. Jarman, *The Guinness Dictionary of Poisonous Quotes*, 1991

APHRA BEHN
With Dryden she vied in indecency and was not overcome.
– **Dr John Doran**

All women together ought to let flowers fall upon the tomb of Aphra Behn, for it was she who earned them the right to speak their minds.
– **Virginia Woolf**

I don't regard Brecht as a man of iron-grey purpose and intellect, I think he is a theatrical whore of the first quality.
– **Peter Hall** quoted in F. Muir, *The Frank Muir Book*

For me the two playwrights to be avoided at all costs are Brecht and Anouilh.
– **Robert Morley**

I admit that, like Wagner, he is a great man: but I can't stand him at any cost.
– **Peter Ustinov**

GEORGE VILLIERS, 2ND DUKE OF BUCKINGHAM

A man so various that he
    seemed to be,
Not one, but all mankind's
    epitome.
– **John Dryden** *Absalom and Achitophel*, 1681

WILLIAM CONGREVE

Wickedness is no subject for comedy: to forget this was Congreve's greatest error, and almost peculiar to him.
– **Samuel Taylor Coleridge**

Mirabel, the fine gentleman

of *Way of the World* is, I believe, not far distant from the real character of Congreve. – **Thomas Davies** *Dramatic Miscellanies*, 1785

William Congreve is the only sophisticated playwright England has produced; and like Shaw, Sheridan and Wilde, his nearest rivals, he was brought up in Ireland.
– **Kenneth Tynan** *Curtains*, 1961

He spoke of his works as trifles that were beneath him, and hinted to me at our first conversation that I should visit him upon no other foot than that of a gentleman who led a life of plainness and simplicity. I answered that had he been so unfortunate as to be a mere gentleman, I should never have come to visit him, and I was very much disgusted at so unseasonable a piece of vanity.
– **Voltaire** *Letters Concerning the English Nation*, 1733

CORNEILLE

Corneille is to Shakespeare

as a clipped hedge is to a forest. – **Samuel Johnson** *Rambler*, No. 60

JOHN DRYDEN

His mind was of a slovenly character – fond of splendour, but indifferent to neatness. Hence most of his writings exhibit the sluttish magnificence of a Russian noble, all vermin and diamonds, dirty linen and inestimable sables. – **Thomas B. Macaulay** 'John Dryden', *Edinburgh Review*, January 1828

EURIPIDES

A cliché anthologist and maker of ragamuffin manikins. – **Aristophanes**

GEORGES FEYDEAU

Without the right timing Feydeau falls flat on his face. – **Alexander Woollcott**

LADY GREGORY

Now that the Abbey Players are world-renowned, I begin to realise that with such an audience and such actors an author is hardly needed. Good acting covers a multitude of defects. It explains the success of Lady Gregory's plays. – **Oliver St. John Gogarty**

LILLIAN HELLMAN

She writes like an angel, but she's a dreary bore as spinach is a dreary bore. I say she's spinach and the hellman with her. – **Tallulah Bankhead** (Hellman had refused to join Bankhead in supporting the cause of Finland against Stalin during World War II.)

VICTOR HUGO

The lighthouse in a sea of absurdity. – **Friedrich Nietzsche** *The Twilight of the Idols*, 1899

EUGENE IONESCO

For me the theatre is most often a confession. The admissions I make are incomprehensible to the deaf; but what else can I do. – **On himself**

BEN JONSON

He killed Mr Marlow, the poet, on Bunhill, coming from the Green-Curtain play-house. – **John Aubrey** *Brief Lives*

A great lover and praiser of himself, a contemner and scorner of others, given rather to lose a friend than a jest, jealous of every word and action of those about him. – **William Drummond** *Conversations with Jonson*, 1842

He was not only a professed imitator of Horace, but a learned plagiary of all the others; you track him everywhere in their snow. – **John Dryden** *Essay Of Dramatick Poesie*

I can't read Ben Jonson, especially his comedies. To me he appears to move in a wide sea of glue. – **Alfred Tennyson** quoted in *Alfred Lord Tennyson, A Memoir by His Son*, 1897

Every half quarter of an hour a glass of Sack must be sent into his Guts, to tell his Brains they must come up quickly, and help out with a line. – **Robert Wilde** *The Benefice*

GEORGE S. KAUFMAN
It was not his own but the pottiness of the world that begloomed him, that gave the Kaufman pompadour the look of the first plume of the hearse.

What can a witty man do but hang his head in a land that has resolutely turned its back on wit, that is ready to cry sabotage to satire, that has traded in its once famous slapstick for a global sceptre. – **Ben Hecht** 'Kaufman', *The Bedside Phoenix Nest* (ed. M. Levin), 1965

A morning glory climbing a pole. – **Alexander Woollcott** attrib. quoted in H. Teichmann, *George S. Kaufman*, 1972

CLARE BOOTHE LUCE
No woman of our time has gone further with less mental equipment. – **Clifton Fadiman**

MAURICE MAETERLINCK
The joy of every parodist. – **George Bernard Shaw**

DAVID MAMET
Mamet has a miraculous ear for the heightened music of

American dialect – it makes poetry out of common usage. – *New York Post*, 1991

CHRISTOPHER MARLOWE

Marlowe . . . was perhaps good enough to make it possible to believe that if he had been born thirty years ago, he might now be a tolerable imitator of Mr Rudyard Kipling.
– **George Bernard Shaw** *Saturday Review*, 25 May 1895

He is the true Elizabethan blank-verse beast, itching to frighten other people with the superstitious terrors and cruelties in which he does not himself believe, and wallowing in blood, violence, muscularity of expression, and strenuous animal passion as only literary men do when they become thoroughly depraved by solitary work, sedentary cowardice, and starvation of the sympathetic centres. It is not surprising to learn that Marlowe was killed in a tavern brawl: what would be utterly unbelievable would be his having succeeded in stabbing anyone else.

– **George Bernard Shaw** 'The Spacious Times', July 1896; *Dramatic Opinions and Essays*, Vol. II, 1909

The first English poet whose powers can be called sublime was Christopher Marlowe.
– **Algernon Swinburne** *The Age of Shakespeare*, 1879

It so happened that at Deptford, a little village about three miles distant from London, as he went to stab with his poynard one named Ingram, that had invited him thither to a feast, and was then playing at tables, he quickly perceyving it, so avoyded the thrust, that withal drawing out his dagger for his defence, he stabbed this Marlowe in the eye, in such sort, that his braines comming out at the dagger's point, hee shortly after dyed.
– **William Vaughan** *Golden Grove*, 1600

MUSTAPHA MATURA

What makes Mustapha Matura our finest dramatist of West Indian origin? A wry humour, a warmth

of feeling, a knack for observing human oddity and for embodying it in quirky, unpredictable dialogue, and the fundamental seriousness with which he writes of people who, like himself, have in some sense become severed from their roots.
– **Benedict Nightingale** *The Times*

SOMERSET MAUGHAM
(ON HIMSELF)
My world popularity is the most interesting thing about me. – Quoted in T. Morgan, *Somerset Maugham*, 1980

(BY OTHERS)
Willie Maugham has a stop-watch by his side and, on completion of the day's quota, goes to the terrace and prepares for the elaborate ritual of the dry martini. – **Cecil Beaton** *The Strenuous Years*

Somerset Maugham hated people more easily than he loved them; I love people more easily than I hate them. That is the difference between me and Somerset Maugham. – **Noël Coward**

Two fundamental failings rob him of greatness. His works do not suggest those 'mysteries' which, as Proust puts it, 'have their explanation probably only in other worlds and a presentiment of which is precisely what moves us most in life and art'. His other fault is the fear of appearing old-fashioned.
– **William Gerhardie** *Memoirs of a Polyglot*, 1925

He was offered a knighthood but when I asked him why he had not accepted he replied: 'They knight jockeys now.'
– **Godfrey Winn** quoted in D. Richards, *The Curtain Rises*, 1966

ARTHUR MILLER
I always preferred *This is Your Life* as a television show.
– **Noël Coward** to Claudette Colbert at the Broadway first night of *After the Fall*

MOLIÈRE
Of all dramatists, ancient and modern, Molière is perhaps that one who has borne most constantly in

mind the theory that the stage is a lay pulpit, and that its end is not merely amusement, but the reformation of manners by means of amusing spectacles. – **George Saintsbury** *A Short History of French Literature*, 1882

Molière had cruel enemies, especially among the inferior writers of the day and their cliques. He also aroused the opposition of the pious, who accused him of writing scandalous books. He was charged with having exposed the characters of powerful persons in the characters of his plays, whereas he had done nothing but hold up views in general for the reprobation of mankind. He would have suffered punishment as a result of these accusations had not Louis XIV, who had encouraged and supported Racine and Despreaux, likewise protected him.
– **Voltaire** *Life of Molière*

He had ambitions to play tragedy, but in this field was not successful. He was exceedingly voluble in speech and had a sort of hiccough which was quite unsuitable to serious roles. This, however, only served to make his acting in comedy more enjoyable. – Ibid.

TOM MURPHY
It has been possible for Tom Murphy to do things which are of enormous significance to theatre as a whole; to write tragedy when many argued that tragedy can no longer be written; to restore a religious sense . . . to move beyond absurdity . . . and to produce theatrical images of transformation at a time when the world seems all too fixed and inescapable . . . It is this which makes him a great playwright.
– **Fintan O'Toole**

EUGENE O'NEILL
Though he possesses the tragic vision, he cannot claim the tragic tongue.
– **John Mason Brown**

He'll probably never write a good play again.
– **George Bernard Shaw on** hearing that O'Neill had

given up drinking; quoted in A. and B. Gelb, *O'Neill*

O'Neill gave birth to the American theatre and died for it. – **Tennessee Williams** quoted in A. and B. Gelb, *O'Neill*

JOHN OSBORNE
No leader of thought or ideas. A conceited, calculating young man blowing a little trumpet.
– **Noël Coward** *Diaries*, 5 May 1959

ARTHUR WING PINERO
His eyebrows look like the skins of some small mammal just not large enough to be used as mats.
– **Max Beerbohm**

HAROLD PINTER
The meaningfulness of a Pinter play is not in its conclusion but in its journey – each pause is a halt on the way to darkness.
– **Gareth Lloyd Evans** quoted in D. Richards, *The Curtain Rises*, 1966

LUIGI PIRANDELLO
The relentless pessimism that pervades his work was best articulated by a character in the short story 'The Deathwatch': 'I'm not suffering on my account, or on your account. I'm suffering because life is what it is.'
– **William Rose Benét** *Reader's Encyclopaedia*, 1948

JEAN-PAUL SARTRE
He is his decade's foremost theatrical confidence man, which in view of the competition is no mean achievement . . . His fecundity in such directions as philosophy, politics, sociology, the novel, the short story, the cinema and the drama is that of a rabbit, yet he seems to operate under the delusion that his reproductions are not rabbits but lions and tigers, whereas even the rabbits he factually delivers himself of are of the mechanical toy variety, stuffed with the sawdust of borrowed ideas.
– **George Jean Nathan** *The World of George Jean Nathan* (ed. C. Angoff), 1952

FRIEDRICH SCHILLER
He razed mental Bastilles.
– **Heinrich Heine** *The Romantic School*, 1836

TOM STOPPARD
(ON HIMSELF)
For me it is such a relief to get an idea!

I write plays because dialogue is the most respectable way of contradicting myself.

JOHN VANBRUGH
The general opinion is that he is as sprightly in his Writings as he is heavy in his Buildings. – **Voltaire** *Letters Concerning the English Nation* (Vanbrugh was an architect as well as a dramatist.)

ORSON WELLES
There but for the grace of God goes God.
– **Herman J. Mankiewicz** (Mankiewicz was co-writer of *Citizen Kane* but Welles tried to get his name taken off the credits.)

THORNTON WILDER
(ON HIMSELF)

I would love to be the poet laureate of Coney island. I would feel enormous satisfaction in being regarded as the voice of the average American.
– Quoted in *New York Journal*, 1 1 November 1955

(BY OTHERS)
A strange mixture of poet, prophet, hummingbird and gadfly. – **Alexander Woollcott** *c.*1933; quoted in S. H. Adams, *A. Woollcott: His Life and His World*, 1945

WILLIAM WYCHERLEY
In truth Wycherley's indecency is protected against the critics as a skunk is protected against the hunters. It is safe because it is too filthy to handle, and too noisesome even to approach.
– **Thomas Macaulay** *Critical and Historical Essays: On the Comic Dramatists of the Restoration*, 1843

He appears to have led, during a long course of years, that most wretched life, the life of a vicious old boy about town. – Ibid.

As King Charles was extremely fond of him upon account of his wit, some of the Royal Mistresses set no less value upon Those Parts in him, of which they were more proper judges.
– **Major Richardson Pack** 1719

See also: Beaumont and Fletcher, Chekhov, Noël Coward, Ibsen, Shakespeare, George Bernard Shaw, Oscar Wilde, Tennessee Williams.

PREJUDICE

No man, being forbidden to do so, shall converse with the wife of another man. But this shall not apply to the wives of actors. – **The Code of Manu** VIII, *c.* AD 100

Concerning players, we have thought fit to excommunicate them so long as they continue to act.
– **Decree of the First Council of Arles** AD 314

All bearwards, common players of interludes, counterfeit Egyptians etc., shall be taken, adjudged and deemed rogues, vagabonds and sturdy beggars.
– **Act of Parliament** 1597

All stage-players and players of interludes and common plays are hereby declared to be, and are, and shall be taken to be rogues . . . whether they be wanderers or no, and notwithstanding any licence whatsoever from the king or any person or persons to that purpose.
– **Ordinance of Parliament** 9 February 1647

No actors, or dogs, or Jews.
– **Notice** outside Hollywood in the early years of the 20th century

Critics are forever discovering homosexual references in my plays where they don't exist.
– **Edward Albee** 1983

'Tis as hard a matter for a pretty woman to keep herself honest in a theatre, as 'tis for an apothecary to keep his treacle from the flies in hot weather; for every libertine in the audience will be buzzing about her honey-pot. – **Thomas Brown** quoted in J. H. Wilson, *All the King's Ladies*, 1958

One should never take one's daughter to a theatre. Not only are plays immoral; the house itself is immoral.
– **Alexander Dumas** *fils*

THE PRESS

Some are born great, some achieve greatness, and some hire public relations officers.
– **Anonymous**

I don't care what you say about me, as long as you say something about me, and as long as you spell my name right. – **George M. Cohan**

Don't ever believe anyone who says a bad press doesn't really hurt. You just have to find ways of coping with it.
– **Peter Hall** *Diaries* (Foreword), 1982

No one ever won an interview.– **Laurence Olivier** quoted in J. Osborne, *Almost a Gentleman*, 1991

If you just say nothing there is no way they can make you talk. – **Twiggy**

Every actor in his heart believes everything bad that's printed about him.
– **Orson Welles**

There is much to be said in favour of modem journalism. By giving us the opinions of the uneducated, it keeps us in touch with the ignorance of the community.
– **Oscar Wilde**

There is only one thing in the world worse than being talked about, and that is not being talked about.
– **Oscar Wilde** *The Picture of Dorian Grey*, 189 1

PRODUCERS

The only way a producer can make an actress great is to marry her.
– **Traditional saying**

Impresario – a promoter with a cape. – **L. L. Levinson**

The theatre will only

triumph when all producers are dead!
– **Joan Littlewood** quoted in T. Cole and H. Chinoy, *Directors on Directing*, 1976

PRODUCERS
– Individuals

GEORGE M. COHAN
He was the boy owner of the American flag, and throughout his life he was the Yankee Doodle Boy.
– **Ward Morehouse** *George M. Cohan*, 1943

JED HARRIS
A strange, paradoxical creature, fated to destroy everything he loves, including himself.
When I die, I want to be cremated and have my ashes thrown in Jed Harris's face.
– **George S. Kaufman**

DAVID MERRICK
He displayed a sneaky knack for extending the life of a production beyond the reasonable expectations of the playwright's mother.
– **Walter Kerr**

If there is any serious doubt that David Merrick is one of the greatest showmen in Broadway history, it can be dispelled by the fact that his flops are as fabled as his hits.
– **Frank Rich** *New York Times*, 1960

BILLY ROSE
Without his name in the paper, Billy felt nude.
– **Ben Hecht** *A Child of the Century* Vol. V, 1954

FLORENZ ZIEGFELD
He introduced into the American theatre an era of lavishness and glamour that has never been surpassed.
– **Eddie Cantor** *Take My Life*, 1957

He was the kind of fellow who made people feel honoured to have him owe them money.
– **Buddy De Sylva** quoted in Eddie Cantor, *Take My Life*, 1957

Do a good show every night because Ziegfeld may be out front. – **Broadway saying**, still used long after Ziegfeld's death

PROLOGUES

Prologues precede the piece in
mournful verse,
As undertakers walk before
the hearse.
– **David Garrick** Prologue to
The Apprentice

The drama's laws the drama's
patrons give.
For we that live to please must
please to live.
– **Samuel Johnson** Prologue
for the opening of Drury
Lane Theatre, 1747

PROMPTS

The players conne not their
parts without book, but are
prompted by one called the
Ordinary, who followeth
at their back with the book
in his hand, and telleth
them softly what they must
pronounce aloud.
– **Richard Carew** *The Survey*
of Cornwall, 1602

PURPOSE

The theatre, like the plague,
is a crisis which is resolved
either in death or in the
return to complete health.
– **Antonin Artaud**

Theatre is the first serum
that man invented to protect
himself against the sickness
of despair. – **Jean-Louis**
Barrault *Nouvelle Reflexions*
sur le Theatre

I'm not a postman . . . I don't
deliver messages.
– **Brendan Behan** when
interviewed on BBC TV
about the meaning of his
plays; quoted in G. Snell,
The Book of Theatre Quotes,
1982

All art is a challenge to
despair.– **D. C. Bentley**
The Life of the Drama, 1965

The purpose is to take
you beyond day-to-day
ambitions and remind you
of your potential. – **Steven**
Berkoff *Sunday Express*
Magazine, 9 August 1992

All arts contribute to
the greatest art of all:
Lebenskunst – the art of
getting through fife.
– **Bertolt Brecht**

Hard political people don't like the theatre, because they think plays get muzzy and ideologically unsound.
– **Howard Brenton** *The Times*, 13 April 1992

The theatre should be necessary – like a bank or a grocer's shop. It should provide something that people cannot get anywhere else. – **Peter Brook** *Observer*, 1970

The business of plays is to recommend virtue, and discountenance vice.
– **Jeremy Collier** *A Short View of the Immorality and Profaneness of the English Stage*, 1698

A play should give you something to think about. When I see a play and I understand it for the first time, then I know it can't be much good. – **T. S. Eliot** *New York Post*, 1963

I am weary up to retirement of seeing plays which deal with the mentally sick and the spiritually infirm. I'm sick and tired of being scolded and told I have no compassion. – **Helen Hayes**

The actor in his turn scatters blessings. He passes the benediction on. He is part of the healing fraternity.
– **Bernard Miles** quoted in D. Richards, *The Curtain Rises*, 1966

The office of drama is to exercise, possibly to exhaust, human emotions. The purpose of comedy is to tickle those emotions into an expression of light relief; of tragedy, to wound them and bring the relief of tears.
– **Laurence Olivier** *Reflections of an Actor*, 1984

A play is not to show occurrence's that happen every day, but things just so strange, that though they never did, they might happen. – **Richard Brinsley Sheridan** *The Critic*, 1779

I don't think any writer has much purpose back of him unless he feels bitterly the iniquities of the society he lives in.
– **Tennessee Williams**

If there is any one thing for all the cast to remember it is the primary aim of the play: the making of 'poetic reality' in which everything occurs with the ease and spontaneity of occurrences in life, no matter how long and carefully the play has been planned and written with that objective in mind.
— **Tennessee Williams** letter to **Bette Davis** about *Night of the Iguana*, 1961

QUICK THINKING

Mr Wood seems rather thin skinned about his Bottom.
— **Newspaper comment** on an actor's reaction to criticism of his acting in *A Midsummer Night's Dream*, quoted in J. Aye, *Humour in the Theatre*, 1932

It's no good looking up your entrance – you missed it!
— **Robert Atkins** directing *A Midsummer Night's Dream* at Regent's Park Open Air Theatre, to a 'fairy' he found sitting with her head between her knees when she should have been on stage

Madge Kendal complained that Sarah Bernhardt's roles were often too 'passionate' for her to bring her daughter to see.
Sarah Bernhardt: Madame, had it not been for passion you would have no daughter to bring.

James Agate to **Lilian Braithwaite**: For a long time I have wanted to tell you I regard you as the second-best actress in London.
Lilian Braithwaite: I'm so flattered to hear that – from the second-best drama critic in London.

No one I know darling.
— **Coral Browne** on seeing the 10-foot-high golden phallus designed for the National Theatre production of *Oedipus* 1968

It [Olivier's sword] flew straight into **Lilian Baylis**'s stage box, nearly killing one of the governors. Everybody was trying to contain their laughter, but the problem was that the stage fight could not continue without the sword. I crawled offstage and hid behind the box, hoping for it to be handed to me, but the governor was too stunned to retrieve it. After what seemed like an eternity, I heard Miss Baylis say, 'Oh give them back the sword, so they can finish and we can all go home'. – **Stuart Burge** on an incident during *Hamlet* at the Old Vic, 1937

Lady Diana Cooper (who starred as a non-speaking statue in the religious drama *The Miracle*) to **Noël Coward**: Didn't you write *Private Lives*? Not very funny. **Noël Coward**: Weren't you in *The Miracle*? Very funny indeed.

Then lead the way, good
 Father, And Heavens so
 shine,
I can't remember another
 blessed line.
– **Mrs Guinness,** exiting after drying while playing Olivia in *Twelfth Night*, quoted in C. Benson, Mainly Players 1926 (Also attributed to **Julia Marlowe**)

Arrogant Actor: Last night **I** was a sensation. I had the audience glued to their seats. **George Jessel:** How clever of you to think of it.

I'm going to fall back on the casting couch. – **Maureen Lipman** when asked for her contingency plans if she failed as an actress

Ladies and gentlemen, if you will allow me to finish the play, I will go home and learn how to act.
– **Edward Sothern** 1852, after being booed during the Boston production of *The Heir at Law*

Madam, if you are invited to play golf you do not take your tennis racquet.
– **Donald Wolfit** response to being asked how he did not mix up his many Shakespearean roles; quoted in R. Harwood, *Donald Wolfit*, 1971

REALISM

Realistic? But the stage is art. Kramskoy has a picture on which the faces are painted beautifully. What would happen if one cut out the nose of one of the faces and substituted a real one for it? The nose would be realistic. But the picture would be ruined. – **Anton Chekhov** quoted in M. Billington, *The Guinness Book of Theatre Facts and Feats*, 1982

RECOGNITION

Photographer at the reception for Noël Coward's play *Pacific*, 1860: Could you please tell me your name? **Noël Coward**: I recommend you to *Who's Who* – and hell. – Quoted in D. Richards, *The Wit of Noël Coward*

It is time that some official recognition were shown of his achievement in keeping the British flag flying over Ruritania. – *Evening Standard*, 1951; comment after the death of **Ivor Novello**

REHEARSALS

There was the usual actors' fussing – like dogs walking round and round a place where they going to sleep. – **Peter Hall** *Diaries*, 19 November 1974

Most playwrights at rehearsals are as much use as a father, all masked-up and sterilized, at the delivery of a child. – **John Osborne** *Almost a Gentleman*, 1991

REPUTATION

Hard by the Mall lives a wench call'd Nell,
King Charles the Second he kept her.
She hath got a trick to handle his pr—,
But never lays hands on his sceptre.
– **Anonymous** poem on actress Nell Gwynne, mistress of Charles II

This agreeable actress (Peg Woffington) in the part of Sir Harry coming into the Greenroom said pleasantly,

In my conscience,
I believe half the men in
the House take me for one
of their own sex. Another
actress reply'd,
It may be so, but in my
conscience, the other half
can convince them to the
contrary.
– **W. R. Chetwood** *A General
History of the Stage*, 1749

Discretion contributed not a
little to make her the Cara,
the Darling of the Theatre;
for it will be no extravagant
thing to say, scarce an
audience saw her that were
less than half of them
lovers, without a suspected
favourite among them.
– **Colley Cibber** on Anne
Bracegirdle, 'The Romantick
Virgin', in *Apology for
the Life of Colley Cibber,
Comedian*, 1740

RESTING

Don't be depressed . . . you
are only gathering strength
for the next spring.
– **Harley Granville Barker**
quoted in D. Blakelock,
Advice to a Player, 1958

RESTORATION
THEATRE

Restoration theatre gives
me the overwhelming
impression of a sex-
orientated, fashionable club:
the Playboy Club of the day.
– **Peter Hall** *Diaries*,
20 August 1977

RALPH
RICHARDSON

(ON HIMSELF)
Has anyone seen a talent?
Not a very big one, but I
seem to have mislaid it.
– **Ralph Richardson** to his
fellow actors after reading
the vicious reviews of his
1952 Hamlet

(BY OTHERS)
Nature . . . has unkindly
refused him any tragic
facilities whatever. His
voice has not a tragic note
in its whole gamut. . . . He
cannot blaze. He saws away
at his nether lip with the
enthusiasm of a Queen's Hall
fiddler or a maniac reducing
a torso to its minimum.
– **James Agate** 1938 on

Richardson's Othello;
quoted in G. O'Connor,
*Ralph Richardson: An Actor's
Life*, 1982

A year or two ago
Richardson had the habit of
acting all his parts with his
buttocks.
– **James Agate** *Ego 1*, 1935

I don't know his name but
he's got a face like half a
teapot. – **George VI**

SCENERY AND
LIGHTING

Irving of course stuck to
gaslight, subtler and more
magical than the electric;
it restricted the painter's
palette but was alive and
imperceptibly a-quiver;
it interposed a film of
waving air between actor
and spectator. – **William
Bridges-Adams** quoted in R.
Speaight, *A Bridges-Adams
Letter Book*, 1971

One evening at Althorp
when Garrick was about
to exhibit some particular
stage-effect of which they

had been talking, a young
man got up and placed
candles on the floor, that
the light be thrown on his
face as from the lamps in the
theatre. Garrick, displeased
at this officiousness,
immediately sat down again.
– **Samuel Rogers** on a visit
by Garrick to Lord Spencer
at Althorp; quoted in *Table
Talk*, 1856

What child is here, that
coming to a play and seeing
Thebes written in great
letters on an old door, doth
believe that it is Thebes?
– **Sir Philip Sidney** quoted in
D. Cook, *A Book of the Play*,
1876

SHAKESPEARE

(ON HIMSELF)
*Alas! 'tis true I have gone here
    and there,
And made myself a motley to
    the view,
Gored mine own thoughts,
    sold cheap what is most
    dear,
Made old offenses of
    affections new.*
– *Sonnet CX*, 1609

Whaur's yer Wully
Shakespeare noo?
– **Anonymous Scottish
theatregoer** on the first night
of the Scottish play *Douglas*
by John Home, 1756

Shakespeare, Madam, is
obscene, and, thank God we
are sufficiently advanced to
have found it out.
– **Anonymous American**
quoted by Frances Trollope
in *Domestic Manners of the
Americans*, 1832

I keep saying, Shakespeare,
Shakespeare, you are as
obscure as life is. – **Matthew
Arnold** letter to A. H.
Clough, December 1847

Mr William Shakespeare
was born at Stratford-
on-Avon in the county of
Warwick. His father was a
Butcher, and I have been
told heretofor by some of
the neighbours, that when
he was a boy he exercised his
father's Trade, but when he
killed a Calfe he would do
it in high style, and make a
speech.
– John Aubrey *Brief Lives*

His Comedies will remaine
witt as long as the English
tongue is understood,
for that he handles *mores
hominum* (the ways of
mankind). – Ibid.

Shakespeare is in the
singularly fortunate position
of being, to all intents and
purposes, anonymous.
– **W. H. Auden** *Forewords
and Afterwords*

The only tribute a
French translator can
pay Shakespeare is not to
translate him.
– **Max Beerbohm** 'Hamlet,
Princess of Denmark'
(on Bernhardt's Hamlet),
Around Theatres, Vol. I, 1924

It will, I believe, be
universally acknowledged,
that few authors are so
instructive as Shakespeare;
but his warmest admirers
must confess that his plays
contain much that is vulgar,
and much that is indelicate
. . . It is hoped that the
present publication will be
approved by those who wish
to make the young reader
acquainted with the various

beauties of this writer unmixed with anything that can raise a blush on the cheek of modesty.
– **Thomas and Harriet Bowdler** preface to their expurgated (bowdlerised) edition, *The Family Shakespeare*, 1818

Shake was a dramatist of note;
He lived by writing things to quote.
– **Henry C. Bunner** *Shake, Mulleary and Go-ethe, c.*1884

I have tried lately to read Shakespeare, and found it so intolerably dull that it nauseated me.
– **Charles Darwin**

Shakespeare, who (taught by none) did first impart,
To Fletcher wit, to labouring Jonson art:
He, Monarch-like, gave those his subjects law,
And is that Nature which they paint and draw.
– **John Dryden** Prologue to his version of *The Tempest*, 1667

Those who accuse him

to have wanted learning, give him the greater commendation: He was naturally learned; he needed not the spectacles of books to read nature; he looked inwards, and found her there.
– **John Dryden** *An Essay of Dramatic Poesy* ,1668

I hear a great deal about Shakespeare, but I cannot read him, he is such a bombast fellow.
– **King George II**

Was there ever such sad stuff as a great part of Shakespeare? Only one must not say so! What! What!
– **King George III** quoted by Fanny Burney, *Diary*

The remarkable thing about Shakespeare is that he really is very good, in spite of all the people who say he is very good. – **Robert Graves**

There is an upstart crow, beautified with our feathers, that with his Tiger's heart wrapped in a player's hide, supposes he is well able to bombast out a blank verse as

the best of you; and being an absolute *Johannes factotum*, is in his own conceit the only Shake-scene in a country.
– **Robert Greene** *A Groatsworth of Wit bought with a Million of Repentance*, 1592 (Greene believed Shakespeare had plagiarized his plots.)

I don't really approve in my Puritan soul of moving Shakespeare into a modem period in order to illuminate him. You merely illuminate some things and obscure others.
– **Peter Hall** *Diaries*, 22 November 1973

Homosexuality? No, I know nothing of the joys of homosexuality. My friend Oscar can no doubt tell you all about that. But I must say that if *Shakespeare* asked me, I would have to submit.
– **Frank Harris** attrib.

If we wish to know the force of human genius we should read Shakespeare. If we wish to see the insignificance of human learning we may study his commentators.

– **William Hazlitt** *Table Talk*, 1821–22

The genius of Shakespeare was not to be depressed by the weight of poverty, nor limited by the narrow conversation to which men in want are inevitably condemned; the incumbrances of his fortune were shaken from his mind, as dewdrops from a lion's mane.
– **Samuel Johnson** preface to *The Plays of William Shakespeare* (Johnson himself had been through periods of poverty and deep depression.)

The stream of Time, which is continually washing the fabrics of other poets, passes without injury by the adamant of Shakespeare.
– Ibid.

Shakespeare never had six lines together without a fault. Perhaps you may find seven but this does not refute my general assertion.
– **Samuel Johnson** J. Boswell, *The Life of Samuel Johnson*, 1791

I remember, the players have often mentioned it as an honour to Shakespeare, that in his writing, whatsoever he penn'd, he never blotted out a line. My answer hath been, would he had blotted out a thousand.
– **Ben Jonson** *Timber or Discoverie Made Upon Man and Matter*, 1640

Sweet Swan of Avon.
– **Ben Jonson** *To the Memory of My beloved, the Author, William Shakespeare*, 1628

He was not of an age but for all time. – Ibid.

The trouble with Shakespeare is that you never get to sit down unless you're a king.
– **George S. Kaufman** quoted in H. Teichmann, *G. S. Kaufman: An Intimate Portrait*, 1972

Shakespeare is not our poet – but the world's.
– **W. S. Landor** *To Robert Browning*

When I read Shakespeare I
    am struck with wonder

That such trivial people
    should muse and thunder
In such lovely language.
– **D. H. Lawrence** *When I Read Shakespeare*, 1929

What there was in the world to be done in Shakespearean has largely been done by Shakespeare.
– **Georg Lichtenberg** *Aphorisms*, 1764–99

It matters not to me whether Shakespeare be well or ill acted; with him the thought suffices.
– **Abraham Lincoln** quoted in *Revue des Deux Mondes*

The most important thing to remember about Shakespeare is that he was a writer, working on commission . . . I like to think that if the Bard were alive today he'd be out at the beach in Beverley Hills tapping out 'High Concept' Movies of the Week on his Wang word processor, up to his ruff in cocaine.
– **Maureen Lipman** *How Was It For You?*, 1985

Shakespeare made his heroes

foreigners and his clowns English.
– **H. L. Mencken**

I don't think I should want to know Shakespeare. I know him as well as I want by knowing his plays.
– **Jonathan Miller**

Or sweetest Shakespeare, Fancy's child
Warble his native wood-notes wild.
– **John Milton** *L'Allegro*, 1632

What needs my Shakespeare for his honoured bones
The labour of an age in piled stones?
Or that his hallowed reliques should be hid
Under a starry-pointing pyramid?
Dear son of memory, great heir of fame,
What need'st thou such weak witness of thy name?
Thou in our wonder and astonishment
Has built thyself a live long monument.
– **John Milton** *An Epitaph on the Admirable Dramatic Poet W. Shakespeare*

He seems to have known the world by intuition, to have looked through nature at one glance.
– **Alexander Pope** *Preface to the Works of Shakespeare*

Brush up your Shakespeare,
Start quoting him now.
Brush up your Shakespeare,
And the women you will wow.
– **Cole Porter** song lyric from *Kiss Me Kate*, 1948

With the single exception of Homer, there is no eminent writer, not even Sir Walter Scott, whom I despise so entirely as I despise Shakespeare, when I measure my mind against his plays.
– **George Bernard Shaw** *Dramatic Opinion and Essays*, Vol. II, 1909

Crude, immoral, vulgar and senseless. – **Leo Tolstoy**

Shakespeare's hideous stage clowns were the maggots in his apple.
– **Peter Ustinov**

Shakespeare is a savage with sparks of genius which shine

in a dreadful darkness of
night. – **Voltaire**

This enormous dunghill.
– **Voltaire**

Now we sit through
Shakespeare in order to
recognize the quotations.
– **Orson Welles** attrib.

He had read Shakespeare
and found him weak in
chemistry. – **H. G. Wells**
Lord of the Dynamos

If the copyright had not
expired the royalties from
Shakespeare's works would
have paid off the National
Debt.
– **Ted Willis** House of Lords
22 November 1978; quoted in
F. S. Pepper, *A Dictionary of
Biographical Quotations*, 1985

SHAKESPEARE'S
PLAYS

You give them all you've got
and the author says to you:
'You've given all you've got?
Good. Now, more. Good.
Now more. More, damn you.
More, more! More! Morel'

Until your heart and guts
and brain are pulp and the
part feeds on you, eating
you. Acting great parts
devours you. It's a dangerous
game.
– **Laurence Olivier** *Observer*,
9 February 1969; quoted in
A. Holden, *Olivier*, 1988

ANTONY AND CLEOPATRA
It was a pleasing prospect.
Only I was vile.
– **Tallulah Bankhead** on the
1937 American production

Tallulah Bankhead barged
down the aisle last night as
Cleopatra and sank.
– **John Mason Brown** 1937

Miss Bankhead played the
Queen of the Nil.
– **George Jean Nathan** 1937

AS YOU LIKE IT
A nice little girl in a wood.
– **James Agate** review of
Peggy Ashcroft as Rosalind,
1933

You can't play Rosalind
without a hat and a tree.
– **Peggy Ashcroft** to **Eileen
Atkins**

CYMBELINE

Cymbeline is an unrewarding part, but surely he is more than a testy Father Christmas in cricket pads.

– **Felix Barker** reviewing **Richard Harris** as Cymbeline; *Evening News*, 1957

HAMLET

Ophelia said I deplore
That young Hamlet's
*   becoming a bore.*
He just talks to himself,
I'll be left on the shelf –
Or dead by the end of Act
*   Four.*

– **Anonymous**

I have lately been told by a gentleman who has frequently seen Mr Betterton perform this part of Hamlet, that he observ'd his Countenance (which was naturally ruddy and sanguine) in this scene of the fourth act where his Father's Ghost appears, thro' the violent and sudden Emotions of Amazement and Horror, turn instantly on the Sight of his father's Spirit, as pale as his Neckcloth, when every Article of his Body seem'd to be affected with a tremor inexpressible; so that, had his Father's Ghost actually risen before him, he could not have been seized with more real agonies; and this was felt so strongly by the audience, that the blood seem'd to shudder in their veins likewise, and they in some measure partook of the Astonishment and Horror, with which they saw this excellent actor affected.

– **Anonymous** account of **Thomas Betterton** in *Hamlet*, quoted in *Laureat*, 1740

I have no hesitation in saying that it is the high water mark of English Shakespearian acting in our time.

– **James Agate** on **John Gielgud**'s Hamlet, 1929

Mr Olivier's Hamlet is the best performance of Hotspur this generation has seen.

– **James Agate** 1937

As Ophelia Miss Cherry Cottrell strikes me as being unripe.

– **James Agate** 1937

Richard Burton once drank a quart of brandy during his performance of Hamlet on Broadway. The only visible effect was that he played the last two acts as a homosexual. – **James Bacon**

The goddamndest bore in literature, that pompous ass the ghost.– **John Barrymore**

A hoop through which every very eminent actor must sooner or later jump.
– **Max Beerbohm**

In the matter of soliloquies we cannot accept Hamlet as an unbiased authority. We merely find in him the possible origin of the belief that talking to oneself is a bad sign.
– **Max Beerbohm**

From first to last no-one smiled . . . One laugh in that dangerous atmosphere, and the whole structure of polite solemnity would have toppled down, burying beneath it the national reputation for good manners. – **Max Beerbohm** on **Sarah Bernhardt** as

Hamlet; 'Hamlet, Princess of Denmark', *Around Theatres*, Vol. I, 1924

Imagine this: one night in a dream, the Bard of Avon hits on his finest so far and wakes himself up and supposes himself to be quilling down the necessary notes of the vision. Next morning he reads what he has written: CASTLE SCANDINAVIA BLOKE IN TIGHTS
– **Ken Campbell** *Furtive Nudist*, 1992

He burst forth with the fury of the thunderstorm, making everything give way to his tremendous touches.
– **John Cole** on **Edmund Kean** as Hamlet

John Barrymore to Jimmy Durante: 'You know Jimmy, some day you ought to play Hamlet.'
Jimmy Durante: 'To hell with 'em small towns. New York's the only place for me.'

I saw Hamlet Pr. of Denmark played: but now the old playe began to disgust this refined age; since his Majestie being so long abroad: – **John Evelyn** *Diary*, 26 November 1661

'Indeed Mrs Partridge,' says Mrs Miller, 'you are not of the same opinion with the town; for they are all agreed that Hamlet is acted by the best player who ever was on the stage.'

'He the best player!' cries Partridge with a contemptuous sneer. 'Why, I could act as well as he myself. I am sure if I had seen a ghost, I should have looked in the very same manner, and done just as he did. And then, to be sure, in that scene, as you called it, between him and his mother, where you told me he acted so fine, why, Lord help me! any man, that is, any good man, that had such a mother, would have done exactly the same.'
– **Henry Fielding** discussion of **Garrick**'s Hamlet in the novel *Tom Jones*, 1749

Larry, it's one of the finest performances I've ever seen, but it's still my part.

– **John Gielgud** to **Laurence Olivier** after Olivier's 1937 debut in Hamlet; quoted in William Redfield, *Letters from an Actor*, 1967

My dear fellow, I never saw anything so funny in my life, and yet it was not in the least vulgar.
– **W. S. Gilbert** when asked by Sir Herbert Beerbohm Tree for an opinion of his performance as Hamlet

A pert, ill-mannered, spoiled, bad- tempered boy with little sense and a theatrical temperament.
– **Norman Hapgood** after **Sarah Bernhardt**'s first Broadway performance as Hamlet, January 1901; quoted in Brooks Atkinson, *Broadway*, 1970

More of a Spamlet really.
– **Jason Hillgate** on **Albert Finney**'s Hamlet at the National Theatre in *Theatre*, 1975

The best thing about Ian McKellen's Hamlet is his curtain call.
– **Harold Hobson** *Sunday*

Times, 1971, quoted in D. Rigg, *No Turn Unstoned*, 1982

I confess myself utterly unable to appreciate that celebrated soliloquy in Hamlet beginning 'To be or not to be', and tell whether it be good, bad or indifferent, it has been handled and pawed about by declamatory boys and men, and tom so inhumanly from its living place and principle of continuity in the play, till it has become to me a perfect dead number.
– **Charles Lamb** 1811

The tragedy of tackling a family problem too soon after college. – **Tom Masson**

This evening I am engaged to spend with a foreigner. He is a Dane, unjustly deprived of his father's fortune by his mother's marrying a second time. I have never yet seen him, but I hear that all the world will be there, which I think is a little unfeeling, as he is a little low-spirited sometimes almost to madness. For my part, from what I have heard, I do not think the poor young man will live out the night.
– **Hannah More** letter to her family, 1776

In Leslie Howard's he was the Duke of Windsor out to get Stanley Baldwin and wife, with Winston Churchill playing both Rosencrantz and Guildenstern. In John Gielgud's he was Lord Alfred Douglas having an exciting, melodramatic cup of tea with Beverley Nichols.
– **George Jean Nathan** on two 20th-century interpretations of Hamlet

A leering milk roundsman of Denmark Hill.
– **John Osborne** on his Hamlet at Hayling Island, 1951, in *A Better Class of Person*, 1981

Ralph (Richardson) chatted about Hamlet, telling me it was like the most amazing train and all Albert (Finney) had to do was to get on it and rush along through cuttings, through stations, through tunnels until finally

he reached his destination.
He must not get off at any of
the stations on the way.
– **Ralph Richardson** quoted
by Peter Hall, *Diaries*, 13
October 1975

Prince Hamlet thought Uncle
   a traitor
For having it off with his
   Mater;
Revenge Dad or not?
That's the gist of the plot,
And he did – nine soliloquies
   later.
– **Stanley J. Sharpless** in the
New Statesman; quoted in F.
Metcalf, *Penguin Dictionary
of Humorous Quotations*,
1986

The Tragedy of Hamlet is
a coarse, barbarous piece,
which would not be tolerated
by the basest rabble in
France or Italy . . . one would
think that this work was the
fruit of the imagination of a
drunken savage. – **Voltaire**

The central problem in
Hamlet is whether the critics
are mad, or only pretending
to be mad. – **Oscar Wilde**

HENRY V
Do you know why you're so
good in this part? Because
you are England!
– **Charles Laughton** to
Laurence Olivier, 1937

KING LEAR
A strange, horrible business,
but I suppose good enough
for Shakespeare's day.
– **Queen Victoria**

MACBETH
To mankind in general,
Macbeth and Lady Macbeth
stand out as the supreme
type of all that a host and
hostess should not be.
– **Max Beerbohm**

Simone Signoret's Lady
Macbeth, a conical, bell-
tented matron who moves
on wheels like a draped
Dalek surmounted by a
beautiful Medusa head,
speaks with a monotonous
French accent punctuated
by American vowels. – **Alan
Brien** *Sunday Telegraph*, 1966

I could never bring myself
to play the part of someone
with such curious notions of
hospitality.

– **Edith Evans** quoted in Richard Huggett, *The Curse of Macbeth*, 1981

Saw Macbeth which, though I saw it lately, yet appears a most excellent play in all respects, but especially in divertisement, though It be deep tragedy: which is Strange perfection in tragedy, it being most proper here, and suitable.
– **Samuel Pepys** *Diary*, 8 January 1667

Her Lady Macbeth is more niminy-piminy than thundery blundery, more viper than anaconda, but still quite competent in its small way. – **Kenneth Tynan** on Vivien Leigh in *Macbeth* with Laurence Olivier, 1955

Judging from the banquet, Lady Macbeth seems an economical housekeeper and evidently patronised local industries for her husband's clothes and the servants' liveries, but she takes care to do her own shopping in Byzantium.
– **Oscar Wilde** on Ellen Terry as Lady Macbeth

in Irving's production, 29 December 1888. (The Sargent portrait of Ellen Terry in her Byzantine costume hangs in the National Portrait Gallery, London.)

THE MERCHANT OF VENICE

Any fan of Walt Disney comics could see that he had modelled his appearance on Scrooge McDuck. – **Clive James** reviewing Laurence Olivier as Shylock, 1974

THE MERRY WIVES OF WINDSOR

In the first act alone of *The Merry Wives of Windsor* there is more life and movement than in all German literature.
– **Karl Marx**

A MIDSUMMER NIGHT'S DREAM

To the King's Theatre, where we saw *Midsummer Night's Dream*, which I had never seen before, nor shall ever again, for it is the most insipid, ridiculous play that ever I saw in my life.
– **Samuel Pepys** *Diary*, 29 September 1662

OTHELLO

[Ralph] Richardson killed himself from the start with a disastrous make-up; no man looking like a golliwog can persuade us that he is talking like a god.
— **Harold Hobson**, 1938

I think Shakespeare and Richard Burbage got drunk together one night and Burbage said, 'I can play anything you write, anything at all.' And Shakespeare said, 'Right, I'll fix you, boy!' And then he wrote Othello.
— **Laurence Olivier** quoted in A. Holden, *Olivier*, 1988

Why was not this called 'The Tragedy of the Handkerchief'? Had it been Desdemona's garter, the sagacious Moor might have smelt a rat; but the handkerchief is so remote a trifle, no Booby, on this side of Mauretania, could make any consequence from it.
— **Thomas Rymer** *The Tragedies of the Last Age Considered*, 1678

RICHARD III

In the evening went to see Larry (Olivier) in Richard III. A tremendous evening. I think the greatest male performance I have ever seen in the theatre. Came out moved and highly exhilarated. He is far and away the greatest actor we have. — **Noël Coward** *Diaries*, 21 September 1944

You have to use every sound in your voice for Hamlet. In Richard III I only used three notes. I based it on imitations I'd heard people do of Irving.
— **Laurence Olivier** on his 1944 Richard III; quoted in J. Mortimer, *In Character*, 1983

ROMEO AND JULIET

Mr Olivier plays Romeo as if he were riding a motor-bike.
— Review of **Laurence Olivier** in the 1935 London production; quoted in A. Holden, *Olivier*, 1988

She won all hearts with flower-like, passionate Juliet.
— **John Gielgud** on Peggy Ashcroft, 1935

Romeo and Juliet is a play, of itself, the worst that ever I heard in my life, and worse acted that ever I saw these people do.
– **Samuel Pepys** *Diary*, 1 March 1662

A rotationary movement of the hand, as if describing the revolution of a spinning jenny; multiplied slaps upon his forehead, and manual elevation of his fall hair; repeated knocking upon his own breast and occasional rapping at the chests of others; the opening of his ruffles, like a schoolboy run riot from the playground, and a strange, indistinct groping inside of his shirt, as if in search of something uncommonly minute, filled up the round of his action, while a voice most unmusical, exerted to a harsh and painful screech, afforded the finishing touch to a Romeo decidedly the worst we have ever witnessed on the London boards.
– **The Sun** 1815 review of Edmund Kean in *Romeo and Juliet*

He looked like a coal miner with a tail coming up from the coal face.
– *Sunday Express* 1954; review of Richard Burton as Caliban

Last Tuesday, at the request of Lady S–, who patronized a poor actor, we all went to the play – which was Dryden's Tempest – and a worse performance have I seldom seen. Shakespeare's Tempest, which for fancy, invention, and originality, is at the head of beautiful improbabilities, is rendered by the addition of Dryden a childish chaos of absurdity and obscenity; and the grossness and awkwardness of these poor unskilful actors rendered all that ought to have been obscure so shockingly glaring, that there was no attending to them without disgust. All that afforded me any entertainment was looking at Mr Thrale, who turned up his nose with an expression of contempt at the beginning of the performance, and never suffered it to return to its

usual place till it was ended!
– **Fanny Burney** on Dryden's reworking of *The Tempest* in *Diary*, 20 October 1779

TWELFTH NIGHT

Claire Bloom played Viola like a wistful little Peter Pan who is worried to death about Tinkerbell.
– *Time and Tide*, 1953

I cannot learn it, and if I cannot learn it, Shakespeare did not write it!
– **Donald Wolfit** on Act IV, Scene I in *Twelfth Night* where Feste, as Sir Topaz, mercilessly taunts Malvolio; quoted in R. Harwood, *Donald Wolfit*, 1971

GEORGE BERNARD SHAW

(ON HIMSELF)

I'm too important to be in an anthology.

People must not be forced to adopt me as their favourite author, even for their own good.

I am like a dentist, there is

so much that is wounding about my work.

Arms and the Man was so completely misunderstood that it made my reputation as a playwright.

My only policy is to profess evil and do good.

I lay an eternal curse on anyone who shall now or at any time hereafter, make schoolbooks of my work and make me hated as Shakespeare is hated. My plays were not designed as instruments of torture.

It is an instinct with me personally to attack every idea which has been full grown for ten years, especially if it claims to be the foundation of human society. – **Review**, January 1896 *Dramatic Opinions and Essays*, Vol. I, 1896

My capers are part of a bigger design than you think.

Shakespeare is one of the Towers of the Bastille, and

down he must come.
– **Letter** to Ellen Terry, 27
January 1897

For ten years past, with an
unprecedented pertinacity
and obstination, I have been
dinning into the public head
that I am an extraordinarily
witty, brilliant and clever
man. That is now part of the
public opinion of England;
and no power in heaven or
on earth will ever change it. I
may dodder and dote; I may
potboil and platitudinize;
I may become the butt and
chopping block of all the
bright, original spirits of
the rising generation; but
my reputation shall not
suffer: it is built up fast and
solid, like Shakespeare's,
on an impregnable basis of
dogmatic re-iteration.
– 'Valedictory', 21 May 1898,
*Dramatic Opinions and
Essays*, Vol. II, 1909

I cannot guarantee myself
as the greatest living hokum
merchant, but I am certainly
one of the best ten.
– Quoted in Frank Harris,
Bernard Shaw, 1931

The fact is, I write my plays
mostly on the tops of buses.
– Quoted in Hesketh
Pearson, *Bernard Shaw*, 1942

(BY OTHERS)
You invite Shaw down to
your place because you
think he will entertain
your friends with brilliant
conversation. But before
you know where you are
he has chosen a school for
your son, made your will for
you, regulated your diet and
assumed all the privileges
of your family solicitor,
your housekeeper, your
clergyman, your doctor and
your dressmaker. When he
has finished with everyone
else he incites the children
to rebellion. And when he
can find nothing more to do
he goes away and forgets all
about you.
– **Anonymous hostess**. B.
Cerf, *Shake Well Before
Using*, 1948; quoted in F.
S. Pepper, *Dictionary of
Biographical Quotations*, 1985

*There was a young man of
    Moose Jaw,
Who wanted to meet Bernard
    Shaw;*

When they questioned him,
  'Why?'
He made no reply,
But sharpened an axe and a
  saw.
– **Anonymous** *c.*1918

Shaw's plays are the price we
pay for Shaw's prefaces.
– **James Agate**

Shaw was charming with
one person, fidgety with
two, and stood on his head
with four. – **Stanley Baldwin**
quoted by G. W. Lyttelton,
The Lyttelton–Hart-Davis
Letters, 18 July 1956

He uses the English language
like a truncheon.
– **Max Beerbohm**

Wells was a cad who didn't
pretend to be anything
but a cad. Bennett was
a cad pretending to be a
gentleman. Shaw was a
gentleman pretending to
be a cad. – **Hilaire Belloc**
quoted in J. B. Priestley,
Thoughts in the Wilderness

It is all very well to believe,
as Shaw did, that all
criticism is prejudiced,
but, with Shaw's dramatic
criticism, the prejudice
is more important than
anything else. – **Eric Bentley**

Oh dear me – it's too late to
do anything but accept you
and love you – but when
you were quite a little boy
somebody ought to have said
'hush' just once.
– **Mrs Patrick Campbell**
letter to George Bernard
Shaw, 1 November 19 12

Shaw, someday you'll eat
a beefsteak and then no
woman in London will
be safe. – **Mrs Patrick**
Campbell attrib. (Shaw was
a vegetarian.)

Few are more capable of
having the best of everything
both ways. His spiritual
home is no doubt in Russia;
his native land is the Irish
Free State; but he lives in
comfortable England . . .
He derides the marriage
vow and even at times the
sentiment of love itself; yet
no-one is more happily or
wisely married . . . He is at
once an acquisitive capitalist
and a sincere Communist.

He makes his characters talk blithely about killing men for the sake of an idea; but would take great trouble not to hurt a fly.
– **Winston Churchill** *Great Contemporaries*, 1937

An Irish smut dealer.
– **Anthony Comstock**

Shaw's relations with women have always been gallant, coy even. The number he has surrendered to physically have been few – perhaps not half a dozen in all – the first man to have cut a swathe through the theatre and left it strewn with virgins.
– **Frank Harris** *Bernard Shaw*, 1931

A freakish homunculus germinated outside lawful procreation.
– **Henry Arthur Jones** (rival playwright)

George Bernard Shaw, most poisonous of all the poisonous haters of England, despiser, distorter and denier of the plain truths whereby men live; topsy turvey perverter of all human relationships, menace to ordered social thought and ordered social life; irresponsible braggart, blaring self-trumpeter; idol of opaque intellectuals and thwarted females; calculus of contrariwise; flibbertygibbet pope of chaos; portent and epitome of this generation's moral and spiritual disorder.
– **Henry Arthur Jones**

Shaw's works make me admire the magnificent tolerance and broadmindedness of the English.
– **James Joyce** quoted in G. Griffin, *The Wild Geese*

He is a good man fallen among Fabians. – **Lenin**

That noisiest of all old cocks.
– **Percy Wyndham Lewis** *Blasting and Bombardiering*, 1937

He writes like a Pakistani who has learned English when he was twelve years old in order to become a chartered accountant.
– **John Osborne** letter in the

Manchester Guardian, 1977

Shaw was a good and
brilliant man . . . had
he created Mr Osborne,
he would have relieved
his heavy dullness with
something lovable.
– (Prof) Bert G. Hornback
letter in the *Manchester
Guardian* in response to
John Osborne

Shaw avoided passion almost
as prudently as Coward.
Frigidity and caution
demand an evasive style and
they both perfected one.
– John Osborne *A Better
Class of Person*, 1981

He had goat's eyebrows . . .
and wintry blue eyes, which
reminded me of a dead
chicken.
– Lilli Palmer quoted in
Celebrity Gossip, 1984

A desiccated bourgeois . . .
a fossilized chauvinist, a self-
satisfied Englishman.
– *Pravda* 1924

As an iconoclast he was
admirable, but as an icon
rather less so.

– Bertrand Russell 'George
Bernard Shaw', *Portraits
From Memory*, 1956

I think Shaw on the whole is
more bounder than genius.
– Bertrand Russell review of
Man and Superman, 1904

Sherard Blaw, the dramatist
who had discovered
himself, and who had given
so ungrudgingly of his
discovery to the world.
– Saki

George Too Shaw To Be
Good. – Dylan Thomas
letter to Pamela Hansford
Johnson, October 1933

The more I think you over
the more it comes home to
me what an unmitigated
Middle Victorian ass you
are. – H. G. Wells

An excellent man: he has
no enemies and none of his
friends like him.
– Oscar Wilde quoted
by Shaw in a letter, 25
September 1896

The way Bernard Shaw
believes in himself is very

refreshing in these atheistic days when so many people believe in no God at all.
– **Israel Zangwill**

RICHARD BRINSLEY SHERIDAN

(ON HIMSELF)
When I say an ill-natured thing 'tis out of pure good humour. – Attrib.

When I write in a Hurry I always feel to be not worth reading, and what I try to take Pains with, I am sure never to finish . . .
– **Letter** to David Garrick, 10 January 1778

A man may surely be allowed to take a glass of wine by his own fireside.
– To a friend who remarked on the calm way he sat in the Piazza Coffee House while his theatre was burning to the ground, 1809; quoted in T. Moore, *Memoirs of the Life of R.B. Sheridan*

(BY OTHERS)
Whatever Sheridan has done or chosen to do has been par excellence the best of its kind. He has written the best comedy (The School for Scandal), the best opera (The Duenna), the best farce (The Critic), and the best address (The Monologue on Garrick) and to crown all, delivered the best oration (the famous Begum speech) ever conceived or heard in this country.
– **Lord Byron** quoted in M. Billington, *The Guinness Book of Theatre Facts and Feats*, 1982

Every man has his element: Sheridan's is hot water.
– **Lord Eldon** quoted in Lord Broughton, *Recollections of a Long Life*, 1865

He could not make enemies. If anyone came to request the repayment of a loan from him, he borrowed more. A cordial shake of his hand was a recipt in full for all demands. He could 'coin his smile with drachmas', cancelled bonds with bons mots, and. gave jokes in discharge of a bill.
– **William Hazlitt** 'On the Spirit of Obligations',

New Monthly Magazine, 24
January 1824

Sheridan wrote for the
actor as Handel wrote for
the singer, setting him a
combination of strokes
which, however difficult
some of them may be to
execute finely, are familiar
to all practised actors as the
strokes which experience has
shown to be proper to the
nature and capacity of the
stage-player as a dramatic
instrument.
– **George Bernard Shaw** in
Saturday Review, 27 June
1896

SHOW BUSINESS

There's no business,
Like show business
Like no business I know.
– **Irving Berlin** song lyric
from *Annie Get Your Gun*,
1946

That's what show business
is – sincere insincerity.
– **Benny Hill** *Observer*, 1977;
quoted in J. Green, *The
Cynic's Lexicon*, 1984

In show business you're a
fruit picker. You go where
the work is. – **Orson Welles**
Newsweek, 27 February 1967

SARAH SIDDONS
(ON HERSELF)
Alas, after I became
celebrated none of my sisters
loved me as they did before.
– Quoted in S. Rogers, *Table
Talk*, 1856

(BY OTHERS)
She is sparing in her action
because English nature does
not act much.
– **James Boaden** *Memoirs of
Mrs Siddons*, 1827

I found her the Heroine of a
Tragedy – sublime, elevated
and solemn. In face and
person truly noble, and
commanding; in manners
quiet and stiff; in voice,
deep and dragging; and
in conversation, formal,
sententious, calm and dry.
– **Fanny Burney** *Diary*, 1787

As a stranger, I must
have admired her noble
appearance and beautiful
countenance, and have

regretted that nothing in her conversation kept pace with her promise; and as a celebrated actress, I had still only to do the same. – Ibid.

A sort of radiance comes round her in scenes where strong heroic virtues are displayed. – Ibid.

The beau ideal of acting . . . nothing ever was, or can be, like her.
– **Lord Byron** quoted in R. Manvell, *Sarah Siddons*, 1970

I should as soon think of going to bed with the Archbishop of Canterbury as Mrs Siddons.
– **Lord Byron** attrib.

Damn it, Madame, there is no end to your nose.
– **Thomas Gainsborough** while painting Mrs Siddons's portrait

She was Tragedy personified. She was the stateliest ornament of the public mind. She was not only the idol of the people, she not only hushed the tumultuous shouts of the pit in breathless expectation, and quenched the blaze of surrounding beauty in silent tears but to the retired and lonely student, through long years of solitude, her face has shone as if an eye had appeared from heaven.
– **William Hazlitt**

Madam, you who so often occasion a want of seats to other people, will the more easily excuse the want of one yourself. – **Samuel Johnson** when unable to find an unoccupied chair during a visit from Mrs Siddons, 1783; quoted in J. Boswell, *The Life of Samuel Johnson*, 1791

I smelt blood. I swear that I smelt blood.
– **J. Sheridan Knowles** on Mrs Siddons as Lady Macbeth

Her voice appeared to have lost its brilliancy (like a beautiful face through a veil).
– **Henry Crabb Robinson** *Diary*, 21 April 1812

Sex was out of the question. Although the face and form

were majestically beautiful, it was the mind that 'burned within her' that gave the charm to the Pythoness. – **William Robson** *The Old Playgoer*, 1846

From the moment she assumed the dress she became the character; she never chatted or coquetted by the green-room fire but placed herself where no word of the play could escape her, or the illusion for a moment be destroyed. – Ibid.

She is too grand a thing for me. – **William Siddons** (husband)

Were a Wild Indian to ask me, what was like a queen, I would have bade him look at Mrs Siddons. – **Tate Wilkinson** *The Wandering Patentee*, Vol. IV, 1795

SLIPS OF THE TONGUE

Boiled, rolled Caesar, I present thee with my sword. – **Anonymous actor** intending to address 'Royal, bold Caesar'; quoted in J. De Morgan, *In Lighter Vein*, 1907

You potted snake with ham and tongue. – **Anonymous actress** muddling the line from *A Midsummer Night's Dream*, 'You spotted snake with double tongue'; quoted in J. Aye, *Humour in the Theatre*, 1932

Now children, because you have all been so good today, Mr Thorkelson will read to you from *The Sale of Two Titties*. – **Marie Christiansen** in *I Remember Mama* quoted in P. Hay, *Theatrical Anecdotes*, 1987

Shall I lay surgery upon my Poll? – **Charles Kemble** intending to say 'Shall I lay perjury upon my soul?'; quoted in J. Aye, *Humour in the Theatre*, 1932

Let us retire and seek a nosy cook. – **Lillie Langtry** to a stage lover; quoted in J. De Morgan, *In Lighter Vein*, 1907

STAGE FRIGHT

I used to play always to the exit light or Gents or Ladies, but I never looked at the audience. I found it too frightening.
– **Dirk Bogarde** *By Myself*, Channel 4 TV, January 1992

They say when the lights hit you the pain and the fear go – it's a goddam lie – they don't. – **Judy Garland** quoted by Dirk Bogarde in *By Myself*, Channel 4 TV, 1992

It's as though you have crossed Niagara on a tightrope 250 times and, on the 251st crossing – vertigo. You are convinced you can't move across the stage without falling over. You go rigid from the knees down. You suddenly wonder, why am I doing this?
– **Derek Jacobi** *Sunday Times*, 24 May 1992

STAGE MANAGEMENT

It required a bland, conscientious temperament that expected abuse and never admiration. The best stage-managers are usually women, who bear indignity for the historical necessity of continuity itself.
– **John Osborne** *A Better Class of Person*, 1981

STAR QUALITY

Madame, it will be eight o'clock when it suits you.
– Besotted callboy to **Sarah Bernhardt**

A star is a person who works hard all his life to become well-known and then wears dark glasses to avoid being recognized.
– **Fred Allen** quoted in *The Wit's Dictionary*

The great ones have a little something extra. To love of the theatre, to intelligence and willingness to work, they bring a personal incandescence that cannot be acquired or imitated.
– **Brooks Atkinson** (on **Katherine Cornell**) in *Broadway*, 1970

Trains, dear? We had them stopped on matinee days, naturally.
– **Gladys Cooper** when asked by Dirk Bogarde how she coped with the noise of trains thundering over Hungerford Bridge above the Playhouse Theatre

People are stars in the theatre in direct ratio with how many people want to go to bed with them.
– **Noël Coward** quoted by Daniel Massey on BBC TV, 1 March 1992

When she walks on screen and says 'Hello' people ask, 'Who wrote that wonderful line of dialogue?'
– **Leo McCarey** probably about Ingrid Bergman

He doesn't displace air.
– **Micheal MacLiammoir** on the difference between a good actor and a great actor

Those whom God has touched on the shoulder.
– **Laurence Olivier** quoted in A. Walker, *Vivien*, 1987

Star quality is danger and vulnerability in equal measures.
– **Eric Portman** recalled by Noel Davis

As in a theatre, the eyes of men,
After a well-grac'd actor leaves the stage,
Are idly bent on him that enters next,
Thinking his prattle to be tedious.
– **William Shakespeare** *Richard II*, Act V, Scene 2

And when do you want me to do that little something for which you are paying me so much money?
– **Ellen Terry** to Dion Boucicault (son of the playwright and one of the first theatre directors), after patiently listening to his endless production notes

SUCCESS

For an actress to be a success she must have the face of Venus, the brains of Minerva, the grace of Terpsichore, the memory of Macaulay, the figure of Juno

and the hide of a rhinoceros.
– **Ethel Barrymore** quoted
in George Jean Nathan, *The
Theatre in the Fifties*, 1953

The toughest thing about
success is that you've got to
keep on being a success.
– **Irving Berlin**

My definition of success is
control.
– **Kenneth Branagh** 1987

*Three theatrical Dames,
Eminent and respectable,
Our accents are undetectable
And though we've achieved
     our aims
If they knew what we'd done
In Eighteen Ninety One
They certainly wouldn't have
     made us Dames.*
– **Noël Coward** *The Lyrics of
Noël Coward*, 1965

The only thing that
prevents Celia Johnson
from becoming the greatest
actress of her time is her
monotonous habit of having
babies. – **Noël Coward**

He has so many irons in the
fire that he was never able
to forge any single one into

a weapon with which to
conquer the world.
– **Curtis Dahl** on playwright,
novelist and Professor
of Medicine, Robert
Montgomery Bird

Becoming a Dame hasn't
helped my insecurities; a
title doesn't ensure you're
going to get another job.
– **Judi Dench** *Daily Mail*,
21 January 1992

I may never have been pretty
but I was jolly larky and
that's what counts in the
theatre. – **Edith Evans** *Radio
Times*, 14–20 August 1976

I am not an agricultural
labourer, but I have this
in common with a certain
type of ploughman who in
bygone days was awarded
by the squire with a pair
of corduroy breeches and a
crown piece in each pocket,
in consideration of his
having brought up a family
of fifteen children without
extraneous assistance. I
have been rewarded for
having brought up a family
of sixty-three plays without
ever having to apply to

the relieving officer for parochial assistance. This knighthood I take to be sort of commuted old-age pension.
– **W. S. Gilbert** on receiving his knighthood, 1907. (His partner Arthur Sullivan had received his knighthood 27 years earlier.)

For an actor success is simply delayed failure.
– **Graham Greene** quoted in J. Green, *A Dictionary of Contemporary Quotations*, 1982

Strange how yesterday's commercial plays and films become undisputed artworks of today. A lesson for the over-serious – particularly the over-serious critic who naturally suspects the successful. – **Peter Hall** *Diaries*, 21 March 1973

The morning after an opening the reek of success is as immediately detectable as the reek of failure, with no word said. I remember Larry saying success smelt like Brighton. – **Peter Hall** *Diaries*, 27 January 1977

The fate of a play is decided by knitting. When the lady at the box office is knitting, the play is a flop. But when the prompter can get on undisturbed with knitting her pullover during the performance, then the piece is sure to be a great success.
– **Ferenc Molnár** quoted in P. Hay, *Theatrical Anecdotes*, 1987

Anyone can sympathize with the sufferings of a friend, but it requires a fine nature to sympathize with a friend's success.
– **Oscar Wilde**

TALENT

There is no such thing as a great talent without great will-power.
– **Honoré de Balzac** *La Muse du Departement*, 1843

Always get a good actress – the beautiful girl won't be noticed beyond the third row.– **Tyrone Guthrie** during rehearsals for Sidney Sheldon's *Roman Candle*, 1960

She's O.K. if you like talent.
– **Ethel Merman** on Mary
Martin 1958

We used to have actresses
trying to become stars.
Now we have stars trying to
become actresses.
– **Laurence Olivier**

TECHNIQUE

'My dear Mr Barrymore,
we are extras, not character
actresses.'
– **Female extras** (hired by
John Barrymore to carry
Ophelia's body during his
Hamlet), when urged to look
less like chorus girls and
more like the virgins they
were supposed to portray

Text? Text? I've never heard
of it. What the hell is text?
All I want, laddie, is first the
bizness, then the cues, and I
bet my last bob I get a bread
and butter notice.
– **Jobbing actor** in the 1880s
recalled by Frank Benson,
My Memoirs

It took me a long time to
discover that the key thing

in acting is honesty. Once
you know how to fake that,
you've got it made.
– **Anonymous actor** quoted
in Edmund Carpenter, *Oh,
What a Blow That Phantom
Gave Me!*, 1973

Now, dears, all we can do
is go on our knees and pray
for lust.
– **Lilian Baylis** aiming
to achieve the required
sexuality for *Measure for
Measure*; quoted in F.
Barker, *The Oliviers*, 1953

The artist's personality must
be left in his dressing room;
his soul must be denuded
of its own sensations and
clothed with the base or
noble qualities he is called
upon to exhibit. I once
had an Italian chamber-
maid who, returning one
evening from seeing me in
Phèdre, said: 'Oh Madame
was so lovely that I didn't
recognize Madame.' And no
compliment ever went more
direct to my heart.
– **Sarah Bernhardt** *The Art
of the Theatre*, 1925

My eyes are really nothing in

particula. . . . God gave me boot buttons, but I invented the dreamy eyelid, and that makes all the difference.
– **Mrs Patrick Campbell**

I belong to the bull moose set.

We are people who go to the same vocal teacher in New York.

His name is Alfred Dixon and his lessons are remarkable for their simplicity. We just sit and moo. It does wonders for the voice and it's remarkably easy – once you have learned how to moo.
– **Noël Coward**

He was the first actor I encountered who prepared to make a laughing entrance by going round doing ha-ha! sounds for hours.
– **George Cukor** on Charles Laughton, quoted in G. Lambert, *On Cukor*

Unless you know your character's mind it's a hollow sound you make.
– **Judi Dench** *Sunday Times*, 15 December 1991

I have found that although actors can play any part and shake it off, actresses cannot.
– **Alan Dent** to **Vivien Leigh** 1949 (while Leigh was playing Blanche Dubois); quoted in A. Holden, *Olivier*, 1988

With some of us it isn't luck.
– **Edith Evans** to a young actor who wished her luck before a radio play

As a young actress I always had a rule. If I didn't understand anything I always said it as if it were improper. – **Edith Evans**

Anyone may achieve on some rare occasion an outburst of genuine feeling, a gesture of imperishable beauty, a ringing accent of truth, but your scientific actor knows how he did it. He can repeat it again, and again, and again.
– **Minnie Maddern Fiske** quoted in *Minnie Maddern Fiske. Her views on Actors, Acting and the Problems of Production*, as told to Alexander Woollcott

Breath, note, tone, word.
– **Elsie Fogarty** fundamental thesis of the founder of the Central School of Speech and Drama, London

The only way to arrive at great excellency in characters is to be very conversant with human nature . . . by this way you will more accurately discover the workings of spirit . . . – **David Garrick**

Appear, shine, and, as it were, die. – **Jean Genet** *Reflections on the Theatre*

You have to spin it all out of yourself, like a spider.
– **John Gielgud** 1961

Generally speaking very good impersonators do not make very good actors.
– **John Gielgud** after catching Richard Burton impersonating him; quoted in W. Redfield, *Letters from an Actor*, 1971

Theory is the backwash of success. – **Cedric Hardwicke**

Good actors are good because of the things they can tell us without talking. When they are talking they are the slaves of the dramatist. It is what they can show the audience when they are not talking that reveals the fine actor.
– **Cedric Hardwicke** *Theatre Arts*, 1958

The important thing in acting is to be able to laugh and cry. If I have to cry, I think of my sex life. If I have to laugh, I think of my sex life. – **Glenda Jackson** attrib.

As for me, I find that I act best when my heart is warm and my head is cool.
– **Joseph Jefferson** quoted in Sarah Bernhardt, *The Art of Theatre*

When in doubt, shout – that's the motto.
– **S. Major Jones**, stage manager; quoted in C. Hardwicke, *A Victorian in Orbit*, 1961

Whatever might extend my experience of the various aspects of human nature I regarded as needful and

imperative study. Under this persuasion I braced my nerves to go through the lunatic asylum . . . I took from thence lessons, painful ones, that in after years added to the truth of my representations.
– **William Charles Macready** *Reminiscences and Diaries*, 1875

Childhood can be a great help to an actor. Your emotions are never so wonderfully clear as then.
- **Alec McCowen** *Sunday Times*, 19 January 1992

Any acting that affects and moves an audience is good acting and anything that doesn't, whatever its imposing content or technical dexterity, isn't.
– **George Jean Nathan** *Encyclopaedia of the Theatre*, 1940

Few people, including actors, know much about the matter and even what the few know is open to question. – Ibid.

Acting is just a bag of tricks.
– **Laurence Olivier**

Sometimes the gods inspire a performance, and then the actor can do no wrong, but the actor must also prepare a performance for the night the gods do not attend.
– **Laurence Olivier** to **Charlton Heston**, 1960; quoted in A. Holden, *Olivier*, 1988

You American actors are all like football players. You wait until you have the truth in your arms before you start running with the ball. We English start running when the curtain goes up and hope the truth will catch up with us.
– **Laurence Olivier** to **Anthony Quinn** 1960; quoted in A. Holden, *Olivier*, 1988

It is next to impossible to produce the effect of great suffering without the actor enduring some degree of it.
– **Laurence Olivier** quoted in J. Mortimer, *In Character*, 1983

Acting is like masturbation, one either does it or one doesn't, but one doesn't talk

about it. – **Eric Portman**
when asked by a young actor
about his technique, 1965;
recalled by Noel Davis

The most precious thing in
acting is the pauses.
– **Ralph Richardson** to
a British National Youth
Theatre Group, 1961; recalled
by Alan Allkins

When a part is first put
before me for studying, I
look it over in a general way
to see if it is in Nature, and
if it is I am sure it can be
played. – **Sarah Siddons**

Technique alone cannot
create an image that you can
believe in . . . creativeness is
not a technical trick.
– **Constantin Stanislavski**
An Actor Prepares, 1926

An actor should be
observant not only on the
stage, but also in real life.
He should concentrate with
all his being on whatever
attracts his attention. – Ibid.

To act you must make the
thing written your own. You
must steal the words, steal

the thought, and convey
the stolen treasure to others
with great art.
– **Ellen Terry** quote found
in the fly-leaf of her copy of
Romeo and Juliet used for
the Lyceum production with
Irving, 1882

Later along in years I heard
Ellen Terry sum up in a
sentence this everlasting
distinction between
the actor's art and the
playwright's. 'My boy', she
said to me, 'act in your
pauses. At those moments
you are a creator, not a
servant of playwrights.'
– **Ellen Terry** quoted by
Cedric Hardwicke in *A
Victorian in Orbit*, 1961

Could you oblige us with
a little more light? I think
you may not have realized
that my comedic effects in
this play are almost wholly
grimacial.
– **Maud Beerbohm Tree** to
the director of *The Mask
of Virtue*, who favoured a
gloomy lighting effect

Normally an actor has
two tracks running – the

character you are playing, and a tiny track recording what you are doing and telling you what comes next. When a great actor is very good, the role is taking over. He is allowing something to happen through him.
– **Dorothy Turin** quoted in A. Holden, *Olivier*, 1988

TELEGRAMS

I SEE YOU ANNOUNCE PHYLLIS NEILSON-TERRY AND LESLIE BANKS IN MACBETH. DID YOU EVER SEE ELLEN TERRY AND HENRY IRVING IN HAMLET? OR PERHAPS YOU ONLY SAW THEM IN JULIET AND ROMEO.
– **James Agate** to the *Radio Times*; quoted in A. McGill and K. Thomson, *Live Wire*, 1982

DOCTOR WILL CUT OFF MY LEG NEXT MONDAY. AM VERY HAPPY. KISSES ALL MY HEART.
– **Sarah Bernhardt** to Mrs Patrick Campbell, 1916

PERMISSION TO EXHIBIT LEG? FEE $ 100,000.
– **Manager** of the Pan American Exposition to Sarah Bernhardt after hearing her leg had been amputated

WHICH LEG?
– **Sarah Bernhardt**

TWO TICKETS RESERVED FOR YOU, FIRST NIGHT PYGMALION. BRING A FRIEND. IF YOU HAVE ONE. – **George Bernard Shaw** to Winston Churchill

CANNOT MAKE FIRST NIGHT. WILL COME TO SECOND. IF YOU HAVE ONE. – **Winston Churchill** to George Bernard Shaw

ALL MY PLAYS EXCEPTING CAVALCADE HAVE BEEN VULGARISED, DISTORTED AND RUINED BY MOVIE MINDS. AM NOW MIDDLE-AGED AND PRESTIGE AND QUALITY OF MY WORK ARE MY ONLY ASSETS FOR THE FUTURE THEREFORE HAVE DECIDED HENCEFORWARD NEVER TO SELL FILM

RIGHTS UNLESS I HAVE
ABSOLUTE CONTROL OF
SCRIPT, DIALOGUE, CAST,
TREATMENT, DIRECTOR,
CAMERAMAN, CUTTER
AND PUBLICITY.
CONVINCED PRESENT
LOSS IS FUTURE GAIN.
– **Noël Coward** to his
American manager Jack
Wilson, on Hollywood bids
for rights to *Blithe Spirit*

AM BACK FROM
ISTANBUL WHERE I WAS
KNOWN AS ENGLISH
DELIGHT.
– **Noël Coward** to his private
secretary Cole Lesley

LAST SUPPER AND
ORIGINAL. CAST
COULDN'T DRAW IN THIS
HOUSE.
– **George S. Kaufman** (who
was working for a stock
company in Troy, NY) to his
father

AM WATCHING YOUR
PERFORMANCE FROM
THE REAR OF THE
HOUSE. WISH YOU WERE
HERE. – **George S. Kaufman**
to actor William Gaxton
during a performance of

Kaufman's *Of Thee I Sing*,
1933

YOU MAY AS WELL
START BEING A STAR
IN WILMINGTON AS
ANYWHERE. SO BE GOOD
TONIGHT.
– **Burgess Meredith** to
Lauren Bacall; quoted in A.
McGill and K. Thomson,
Live Wires, 1982

AM CRAZY TO PLAY ST.
JOAN.
– **Anonymous actress** to
George Bernard Shaw

I QUITE AGREE.
– **George Bernard Shaw**

EXCELLENT! GREATEST!
– **George Bernard Shaw**
to **Cornelia Otis Skinner**,
who played in *Candida* on
Broadway, 1935

A MILLION THANKS BUT
UNDESERVING SUCH
PRAISE.
– **Cornelia Otis Skinner** to
George Bernard Shaw

I MEANT THE PLAY.
George Bernard Shaw to
Cornelia Otis Skinner

SO DID I!
Cornelia Otis Skinner to
George Bernard Shaw

NO GIRLS. NO LEGS. NO
JOKES. NO CHANCE.
– **Telegram** sent to Walter
Winchell after the out-of-
town premiere of *Oklahoma*
in Newhaven, 1943

THANK YOU INDEED FOR
YOUR MAGNIFICENT
AND GENEROUS REVIEW
OF MY WORK. MAY I
CONTINUE TO DESERVE
IT OF YOU AND THE
PUBLIC. GARRICK IS
MY YARDSTICK, HE
HAD VERSATILITY AND
A ROUND FACE TOO.
WARMEST REGARDS.
– **Donald Wolfit** to James
Agate

HAVE BEEN LOOKING
ROUND FOR AN
APPROPRIATE WOODEN
GIFT AND AM PLEASED
HEREBY TO PRESENT YOU
WITH ELSIE FERGUSON'S
PERFORMANCE IN HER
NEW PLAY.
– **Alexander Woollcott** to
George S. Kaufman, on his
fifth wedding anniversary

ELLEN TERRY

(ON HERSELF)

I am not a great actress, I
am not indeed. I am only
a very useful one to Henry
[Irving].
– To critic Clement Scott,
after his enthusiastic review
of Faust, 1885

I can pass swiftly from
one effect to another, but I
cannot fix one, and dwell
on it, with that superb
concentration which seems
to me the special attribute of
the tragic actress.
– *Memoirs*, 1908

Though I may seem like
myself to others, I never
feel like myself when I am
acting, but some one else, so
nice, and so young and so
happy, and always-in-the-
air, fight and bodyless.
– Quoted in *Ellen Terry
and Bernard Shaw. A
Correspondence* (ed.
Christopher St. John), 1933

You can get on without
beauty, but it is impossible
for an actress to achieve
any distinction without

Imagination, Individuality and Industry.
– Quoted in R. Findlater, *The Player Queens*, 1976

(BY OTHERS)
She has a voice of plum coloured velvet.
– **James Agate** *Ego 1*, 1935

E. T. was persuadable – especially on Mondays – less so on Tuesdays. On Wednesdays people around her found it difficult to make her understand what it was they were trying to say – but by the time Thursday arrived she could be counted on to do the very thing they didn't expect. Friday she devoted to telling them that it didn't hurt, and that they must be brave and not cry – Saturday was always a half-holiday, spent in promising her advisers she would be good next week – and on Sunday she generally drove away to Hampton Court, waving her lily white hand.
– **Edward Gordon Craig** (son), *Ellen Terry and Her Secret Self*, 1931

Even with her head in a bag

she would have captured the house. – Ibid.

Ellen Terry played but one part – herself, and when not herself she couldn't play it.
– Ibid.

She was large and lovely and gracious and opulent and untidy with everything falling out of her voluminous handbag.
– **Gwen Ffrangcon-Davies** *The Times*, 26 January 1991

Her voice has a sort of monotonous, husky thickness which is extremely touching, though it gravely interferes with the modulation of many of her speeches. – **Henry James** *The Nation*, 12 June 1879

She was an extremely beautiful girl and as innocent as a rose. When Watts kissed her, she took for granted she was going to have a baby.
– **George Bernard Shaw** quoted in S. Winston, *Days with Bernard Shaw*

A heartless waste of an

164

exquisite talent. What a theatre for a woman of genius to be attached to.
– **George Bernard Shaw** on Ellen Terry's partnership with Irving at the Lyceum

The perfect symbol in her work of what the true theatre is – an instrument which transformed body, voice, clothes, words, all materials, into spirit – spiritual essence. – **Sybil Thorndike** quoted in R. Findlater, *The Player Queens*, 1976

Our Lady of the Lyceum.
– **Oscar Wilde**

THE THEATRE

The theatre is not a night-school. Its drama illumines philosophy, sociology, politics and the rest by reflection, in that it lights up the philosopher, the sociologist and the politician. – **James Agate**

The theatre is in reality the Genesis of creation. It will be done. – **Antonin Artaud** letter, 1948

You're not considered seriously in this country [UK] until you've been on the stage and done all that crap.
– **Dirk Bogarde** *By Myself*, Channel 4 TV, January 1992

The theatre must be treated with respect. It is a house of strange enchantment, a temple of dreams.
– **Noël Coward**

To save the Theatre, the Theatre must be destroyed, the actors and actresses all die of the plague . . . they make art impossible.
– **Eleonora Duse** quoted in A. Symons, *Studies in Seven Arts*

It is still only in the theatre that for better or worse, glory or disaster, an actor or actress can make direct contact with an audience, a connection without which they are incomplete as artists. It is in the theatre, above All, that the audience may share the rare magnificence of great acting, an experience of instant excellence, truth and joy

to which there can be no parallel in the cinema or in the television rooms.
– **Richard Findlater** *The Player Queens*, 1976

The theatre is the aspirin of the middle classes.
– **Wolcott Gibbs** *More in Sorrow*, 1958

If all the arts that mankind has Invented to clothe its concept of reality and to ornament its leisure moments, none is more suited to the genius of the female of the species than that of the theatre.
– **Rosamond Gilder** *Enter the Actress*, 193 1

The theatre is ruthless. An actor walks on the stage and within 30 seconds you know whether you want to watch him or not.
– **Peter Hall** *Diaries*, 12 June 1974

The theatre is the best way of showing the gap between what is said and what is seen to be done and that is why, ragged and gap-toothed as it is, it has still a far healthier

potential than some poorer, abandoned arts.
– **David Hare** quoted in the *Penguin Dictionary of Modem Quotations*, 1980

For me, the theatre is the projection on a stage of the interior world.
– **Eugene Ionesco**

Come leave the loathed stage,
And the more loathsome age;
Where pride and impudence
(in faction knit)
Usurpe the chair of wit!
– **Ben Jonson** *Ode* (to himself) 1631; written after his plays had been poorly received

To my mind there is no sadder spectacle of artistic debauchery than a London theatre; the overfed inhabitants of the villa in the stalls hoping for gross excitement to assist them through their hesitating digestions; an ignorant mob in the pit and gallery forgetting the miseries of life in imbecile stories reeking of the sentimentality of the backstairs.
– **George Moore** *Confessions*

of a Young Man, 1888
The stage can be defined as
a place where Shakespeare
murdered Hamlet and a
great many Hamlets have
since murdered Shakespeare.
– **Robert Morse** 1965

The gathering together for
a special occasion is at the
very heart of what theatre is.
– **Adrian Noble** *The Times*,
1 October 1991

The Theatre, for all its noise
and glitter, is a tiny world.
Most of the people who work
in it do not realise how small
it is because they never take
the risk of stepping outside
it. – **J. B. Priestley** 195 1

The stage is actors' country.
You have to get your
passport stamped every so
often or they take away your
citizenship.
– **Vanessa Redgrave**
Newsweek, 10 February 1975

I think the theatre is a
wonderful holiday.
– **Tony Richardson** 1966

A change, slight but
unmistakable has taken
place; the English theatre
has been dragged, as Adlai
Stevenson once said of the
Republican party, kicking
and screaming into the
twentieth century.
– **Kenneth Tynan** *Curtains*,
1961

Whoever condemns the
theatre is an enemy to
his country. – **Voltaire**
letter to the Paris police
commissioner, 20 June 1788

Theatre is a group activity
in public. It is one of the few
public arenas we have left.
It is bold and courageous,
like medieval jousting. A
muscular place where you
get good jokes.
– **Timberlake Wertenbaker**
Guardian, 4 September 1991

Those Enchanted Aisles.
– **Alexander Woollcott**
(book title)

TOURING

Oh, Lilian, I hear you are a
perfect *tour de force* playing
me!
And here I am forced to tour.

– **Mrs Patrick Campbell** to Lilian Braithwaite who was playing a character based on 'Mrs Pat' in Ivor Novello's *Party*; quoted in R. May, *The Wit of the Theatre*, 1969

God was very good to me. He never let me go on tour.
– **Edith Evans**

Fifteen shillings a week could get you bed and breakfast in a place like Glasgow, but you might find yourself enacting the old gag of leaning against the wall in your overcoat to feel the warmth from the fire in the house next door.
– **John Osborne** *A Better Class of Person*, 1981

I remember a landlady who used to split her dining room into two halves: straight actors on the left, variety turns on the right.
– **Ernie Wise** quoted in *Apt and Amusing Quotations* (ed. G.F. Lamb), 1986

Mrs Roosevelt runs the best theatrical boarding house in Washington.
– **Alexander Woollcott** who stayed at the White House while playing in *The Man Who Came to Dinner*

TRAGEDY

Tragedy is an imitation of an action that is serious, complete, and of a certain magnitude, effecting through pity and fear the proper catharsis, or purgation, of emotions.
– **Aristotle** *Poetics I*, c.322 BC

Tragedy represents the life of princes; comedy serves to depict the actions of the people.
– **François D'Aubignac** *La Pratique de Theatre*, c.1660

Sex, flesh, and physicality are the root of tragedy.
– **Dario Fo** *The Independent*, 1 April 1992

HERBERT BEERBOHM TREE

(ON HIMSELF)
Oh my God! Remember you're in Egypt. The *skay* is only seen in Kensington.

– To an over-refined actor, attrib.

I can stand any amount of flattery so long as it's fulsome enough.
– Quoted in M. Beerbohm, *From a Brother's Standpoint*

Ladies –just a little more virginity, if you don't mind.
– While directing a production of Shakespeare's *Henry VIII*; quoted in A. Woollcott, *Shouts and Murmurs*

(BY OTHERS)
Do you know how they are going j to decide the Shakespeare-Bacon dispute? They are going to dig up Shakespeare and dig up Bacon; they are going to set their coffins side by side, and they are going to get Tree to recite Hamlet to them, and the one who turns in his coffin will be the author of the play.
– **W. S. Gilbert** letter, quoted in H. Pearson, *Lives of the Wits*, 1962

His performance as a whole often fell short of high excellence, yet these same impersonations were lit by insight and masterly strokes of interpretation which made the spectator feel that he was watching the performance of the most imaginative of living actors.
– **Desmond MacCarthy** *From the Stalls*, c.1920

With the amount of personal attention, Mr Tree, which you give to all your presentations, and the care you bestow on every detail, I really don't think you need an actual producer. Nor with the constant supervision you so thoroughly exercise, have you any use for a stage manager. What you really require are a couple of tame, trained echoes!
– **Hugh Moss**, after an engagement with Tree; quoted in J. Graham, *An Old Stock Actor's Memories*. (Tree was an old-style actor-manager who produced, acted and directed.)

Even when he was hopelessly miscast Tree's acting was so clever, so inventive, so varied and interesting, that

for unalloyed entertainment one wanted rather to see him in a bad play than anyone else in a good one.
– **Hesketh Pearson** *The Last Actor Managers*, 1950

A charming fellow, so clever: he models himself on me.
– **Oscar Wilde** quoted in H. Pearson, *Beerbohm Tree*, 1956

OSCAR WILDE

(ON HIMSELF)
Who am I to tamper with a masterpiece?
– When asked to make changes to one of his plays

I have nothing to declare but my genius.
– To customs on his arrival in New York, 1882

(BY OTHERS)
The solution that he, deliberately or accidentally found, was to subordinate every other dramatic element to dialogue for its own sake and create a verbal universe in which the characters are determined by the kinds of things they say,

and the plot is nothing but a succession of opportunities to say them.
– **W. H. Auden** *Forewords and Afterwords*, quoted in F. S. Pepper, *Dictionary of Biographical Quotations*, 1985

From the beginning Wilde performed his life and continued to do so even after fame had taken the plot out of his hands. – Ibid.

That sovereign of insufferables, Oscar Wilde, has ensued with his opulence of twaddle and his penury of sense . . . With a knowledge that would equip an idiot to dispute with a cast-iron dog, an eloquence to qualify him for the duties of the caller of a hog-ranch, and an imagination adequate to the conception of a tomcat, when fired by contemplation of a fiddle-string, this consummate and star-like youth, missing everywhere his heaven-appointed functions and offices, wanders about, posing as a statue of himself, and like the sun-smitten image of Memnon, emitting

meaningless murmurs in the blaze of women's eyes.
– **Ambrose Bierce** 'Greetings to an Aesthetic Visitor', *Wasp*, 31 March 1882

Like a many-coloured humming top he was at once a bewilderment and a balance.
– **G. K. Chesterton** *Daily News*, 19 October 1910

Paradox with him was only truth standing on its head to attract attention.
– **Richard Le Gallienne**

Oscar Wilde's talent seems to me essentially rootless, something growing in a glass in a little water.
-- **George Moore**

Oscar and George Bernard Cannot be reconciled. When I'm Wilde about Shaw I'm not Shaw about Wilde.
– **Freddie Oliver**

If with the literate I am Impelled to try an epigram I never seek to take the credit We all assume that Oscar said it.
– **Dorothy Parker**

He had the property of making his critics dull. They laugh angrily at his epigrams, like a child who is coaxed into being amused in the very act of setting up a yell of rage and agony. They protest that the trick is obvious, and that such epigrams can be turned out by the score by anyone lightminded enough to condescend to such frivolity. As far as I can ascertain, I am the only person in London who cannot sit down and write an Oscar Wilde play at will. The fact that his plays, though apparently lucrative, remain unique under these circumstances, says much for the self-denial of our scribes. – **George Bernard Shaw** review, 1895, *Dramatic Opinions and Essays*, Vol. I, 1909

It was rather amusing as it was a complete mass of epigrams, with occasional whiffs of grotesque melodrama and drivelling sentiment.
– **Lytton Strachey** on *A Woman of No Importance*;

letter to Duncan Grant,
2 June 1907

When Oscar came to join his God,
Not earth to earth but sod to sod.
It was for sinners such as this
Hell was created bottomless.
– **Algernon Swinburne**

He was over-dressed, pompous, snobbish, sentimental and vain. But he had an undeniable flair for the possibilities of the commercial theatre. He got himself into trouble, poor old thing, by an infringement of a very silly law, which was just as culpable, and just as boring, as an infringement of traffic or licensing regulations.
– **Evelyn Waugh** *Harper's Bazaar,* November 1930

What has Oscar in common with Art? Except that he dines at our tables and picks from our platters the plums from the puddings he peddles in the provinces.
– **J. M. Whistler** letter to *The World*, 17 November 1886. (Wilde and Whistler were

engaged in a long-running feud. In his reply Wilde wrote 'With our James vulgarity begins at home and should be allowed to stay there.')

They sent Oscar Wilde, that poor man, to Reading Jail for doing what all other actors today get knighted for. – **Wilfrid Hyde White** quoted in D. McClelland, *Star Speak*, 1987

Oscar was not a man of bad character; you could trust him with a woman anywhere. – **William Wilde** (brother), 1895; quoted in H. Pearson, *The Marrying Americans*, 196 1

TENNESSEE WILLIAMS

(ON HIMSELF)
I changed my name to Tennessee Williams, the justification being mainly that the Williamses had fought the Indians for Tennessee and I had already discovered that the life of a young writer was going to

be something similar to the defence of a stockade against a band of savages.

What writers influenced me as a young man? Chekhov! As a dramatist? Chekhov! D. H. Lawrence, too, for his understanding of sexuality, of life in general.

A morbid shyness once prevented me from having much direct communication with people, and possibly that is why I began to write to them plays and stories. But even now, when that first tongue-locking, face-flushing, silent and crouching timidity has worn off with the passage of the troublesome youth that it sprang from, I still find it somehow easier to 'level with' crowds of strangers in the hushed twilight of orchestra and balcony sections of the theatres than with individuals across a table from me . . .
– Introduction to *Cat on a Hot Tin Roof*

I have made a covenant with myself to continue to write, since I have no choice, it is so deeply rooted as a way of existence and a form of flight . . . – Memoirs

My tragedies are funnier than my comedies. Some of these characters have to laugh. They've got to. Or they'll die.

(BY OTHERS)
Mr Williams's problem is not lack of talent. It is, perhaps, an ambiguity of aim; he seems to want to kick the world in the pants and yet be the world's sweetheart, to combine the glories of martyrdom with the comforts of success.
– **Eric Bentley** *New Republic*

Tennessee Williams has a strong streak of poetry, but I think he has run into the ground rather – what with all those neurotic mothers, castrations and things.
– **Noël Coward** quoted in D. Richards, *The Wit of Noël Coward*

He sometimes ran a purple ribbon through his typewriter and gushed

where he should have damned.
– **T. E. Kalem** *Time*, 1983; quoted in C. Jarman, *The Guinness Dictionary of Poisonous Quotes*, 1991

If a swamp alligator could talk, it would sound like Tennessee Williams.
– **Rex Reed** 1972

Playwright Tennessee Williams often writes like an arrested adolescent who disarmingly imagines that he will attain stature if (as short boys are advised in Dixie) he loads enough manure in his shoes.
– *Time Magazine*

– Biographical Index –

British Prime Minister
1923–24, 1924–29, 1935–37
George Bernard Shaw

BALZAC Honoré de 1799–1850
French novelist (*Eugene Grandet*)
Talent

BANCROFT Sir Squire 1841–1926
English actor-manager
Finance

BANKHEAD Tallulah 1903–68
American actress famous for
outrageous behaviour
*Bad Habits; Tallulah Bankhead;
Critical Abuse – plays; Critics
– Alexander Woollcott; Fans;
Finance; First Nights; Insults;
Playwrights – Lillian Heilman;
Shakespeare's Plays - Antony
and Cleopatra*

BANNISTER John (Jock)
1760–1836 English comic actor
Comedy

BARKER Felix 1917–97
British drama critic
Shakespeare's Plays – Cymbeline

BARKER Harley Granville
1877–1946
English writer/actor/director
Resting

BARKER Howard b. 1946
British playwright
Censorship

BARKLEY Alben W. 1877–1956
United States Senator
Audiences

BARNES Clive 1927–2008
British-born American drama
critic; most influential in 1970s
on the *New York Post*
*Critical Abuse – plays; Critics –
Clive Barnes; Plays*

BARNUM Phineas T. 1810–91
American showman and
theatrical producer
Finance

BARRAULT Jean Louis 1910–94
French actor/director
Purpose

BARRIE Sir James 1860–1937
Scottish novelist and dramatist
(*Peter Pan*)
*J. M. Barrie; Critical Abuse –
plays; Method Acting*

BARRYMORE Ethel 1879–1959
American actress; sister of
John and Lionel
Barrymores; Success

BARRYMORE John 1882–1942
American actor; brother of
Ethel and Lionel; famous for
his Hamlet
*Artistic Integrity; Audiences;
Barrymores; Dressing Room
Talk; Fame; Shakespeare's Plays
– Hamlet; Technique*

BARRYMORE Lionel 1878–1954
American actor and musician;
brother of Ethel and John
Barrymores; Epitaphs

BARRYMORE Maurice (Herbert
Blythe) 1847–1905
English actor who took the
name Barrymore from a
playbill and emigrated to
the US; he and Georgina Drew
(1856–93) were parents of Ethel,
John and Lionel

Actors – Maurice Barrymore; Epitaphs

BART Lionel 1930–99
British composer/lyricist/
playwright (*Olivier, Blitz*)
Critical Abuse – plays; Criticism

BAXTER Beverley 1891–1964
English theatre critic
Critics – Kenneth Tynan; Gielgud

BAYLIS Lilian 1874–1937
Founder of the Old Vic and
Sadler's Wells theatres
Fame; Finance; Life; Quick Thinking; Technique

BEATON Sir Cecil 1904–80
English photographer and
stage designer
Actors – Katharine Hepburn; Playwrights – Somerset Maugham

BEAUMONT Sir Francis
1584–1616 English dramatist;
collaborator with Fletcher (*The Maid's Tragedy*)
Beaumont and Fletcher

BEAUMARCHAIS Pierre
Augustin Caron de 1732–99
French dramatist (*The Barber of Seville*)
Audiences

BECKETT Samuel 1906–89
Innovative Irish-born
playwright (*Waiting for Godot*)
Playwrights – Beckett

BEERBOHM Sir (Henry)
Max(imilian) 1872–1956
English writer/caricaturist/
theatre critic; succeeded G. B.

Shaw on *The Saturday Review
Comedy; Critical Abuse –
actors (Duse); Critics – Max
Beerbohm; Criticism; Epitaphs –
Dan Leno; Failure; Playwrights
– Pinero; Shakespeare;
Shakespeare's Plays – Hamlet,
Macbeth;
H. B. Tree*

BEHAN Brendan 1923–64
Irish playwright
Purpose

BEHN Mrs Aphra 1640–89
First English woman to work
as a professional writer and
dramatist (*The Rover*)
Playwrights – Aphra Behn

BELLOC (Joseph) Hilaire
1870–1953 Anglo-French writer
G. B. Shaw

BENCHLEY Nathaniel Goddard
1915–81
American writer
Method Acting

BENCHLEY Robert 1889–1945
American actor/drama critic
(*Life, New Yorker*); member
with Alexander Woollcott
and Dorothy Parker of the
Algonquin Round Table
*Critical Abuse – plays; Critics;
Critics – R. Benchley*

BENET William Rose 1886–1950
American writer
Playwrights – Pirandello

BENNETT Alan b. 1934
English playwright/actor
Critics

BENNETT (Enoch) Arnold

1867–1931 British writer (*The
Old Wives' Tale*)
Actors; *G. B. Shaw*

BENSON Lady Constance
(Constance Featherstonhaugh/
Samuel) 1860–1946 Member of
Sir Frank Benson's Shakespeare
company. Married FB in 1888
Advice; Bad Habits

BENSON Sir Frank 1858–1939
English actor, founder of
the Shakespeare Festival,
Stratford-upon-Avon
*Actors – Frank Benson;
Technique*

BENTLEY E(ric) C. b. 1916
English-born American theatre
critic
Critics; Purpose; G. B. Shaw

BERGMAN Ingrid 1915–82
Swedish actress
Ambition; Star Quality

BERKOFF Steven b. 1937
British actor/playwright
(*Kvetch*)
Purpose

BERLIN Irving 1888–1989
American composer of popular
songs (*God Bless America*) and
musicals (*Annie Get Your Gun*)
*Musicals; Show Business;
Success*

BERNARD Tristan 1866–1947
French playwright
Audiences

BERNHARDT Sarah (Henriette
Bernard) 1844–1923 French
actress, 'The Divine Sarah',
regarded as the greatest

tragedienne of her day
*Actors – Duse; Audiences;
Costume and Make-up;
Finance; Insults; Life; Quick
Thinking; Shakespeare's
Plays – Hamlet; Star Quality;
Telegrams*

BETTERTON Mary c.1637–1712
English actress, the first to be
buried in Westminster Abbey;
married to Thomas Betterton
Actors – Mary Betterton

BETTERTON Thomas 1635–1710
English actor/dramatist;
married to Mary Betterton
Shakespeare's Plays – Hamlet

BETTY William Henry West
(Master Betty) 1791–1874
English child star, 'The Young
Roscius', played Romeo,
Hamlet and Richard III aged
only 12
Actors – Master Betty

BIBESCO Elizabeth 1897–1945
American writer (*Haven*)
Life

BIERCE Ambrose 1842–1914?
American journalist
Playwrights

BIGGE Sir Arthur 1849–1931
Groom in Waiting to Queen
Victoria
Censorship

BIRD Robert Montgomery
1806–54 American playwright/
novelist
Success

BLAKELOCK Denys 1901–70
English actor

Playwrights; Resting

BLOOM Claire b. 1931
English actress
Shakespeare's Plays – Twelfth Night

BOGARDE Sir Dirk (Derek Van Den Bogaerde) 1921–99
British actor/writer
Fans; Stage Fright; Theatre

BOGART Humphrey 1899–1957
American actor and film star
Method Acting

BOORSTIN Daniel J. 1914–2004
American writer
Fame

BOOTH Edwin 1833–93
American actor famous for his Hamlet and Othello
Actors; Actors – Edwin Booth

BOOTH Junius Brutus Sen. 1796–1852 American actor; father of Junius Brutus jun., Edwin and John Wilkes (who assassinated President Lincoln)
Bad Habits

BOOTHROYD Basil 1910–88
British writer and broadcaster
Critics

BOSWELL James 1740–95
Scottish biographer of Dr Samuel Johnson
Actors; Garrick; Shakespeare; Sarah Siddons

BOUCICAULT Dion 1822–90
Irish born dramatist/actor
Epitaphs; Finance; Plays

BOWDLER Thomas 1754–1825
English reformer who, with his sister Harriet, published an expurgated version of Shakespeare's works (*Family Shakespeare*) in 1818, giving rise to the expression 'to bowdlerize'
Censorship; Shakespeare

BRACEGIRDLE Anne c.1663–1748
English actress, brought up by Thomas and Mary Betterton
Actors – Anne Bracegirdle; Reputation

BRADY William A. 1863–1950
American theatrical producer
Finance

BRAGG Melvyn b. 1939
British writer
Failure

BRAHMS Caryl 1901–82
English writer
Beaumont and Fletcher

BRAITHWAITE Dame Lilian 1865– 1940 English actress
Insults; Quick Thinking; Touring

BRANAGH Kenneth b. 1961
British actor/director/producer
Success

BRANDO Marlon 1924–2004
American actor and film star
Acting; Actors; Fame

BRECHT Bertolt 1898–1956
German dramatist/poet with strong Marxist principles
Playwrights – Anouilh; Purpose

BREMONT Comtesse de 1856–1922 American? journalist
Insults

BRENNAN Robert E.
fl. 1930s/40s American writer

Critics – Dorothy Parker
BRENTON Howard b. 1942
British playwright
Avant-garde; Comedy; Plays;
Purpose
BRIDGES-ADAMS William
1889– 1965 English theatre
director
Scenery and Lighting
BRIEN Alan 1925–2008
English journalist and critic
Shakespeare's Plays – Macbeth
(Simone Signoret)
BRIERS Richard 1934–2013
English actor
Acting
BRINDLEY Madge 1901–68
British actress
Critical Abuse – actors
BROOK Peter b. 1925
British theatre director/
producer
Avant-gurde; Directors – Peter
Brook; Gielgud; Purpose;
Technique
BROUGHTON John, 1st Baron
1786– 1869
English politician and writer
Kean
BROUN Heywood C. 1888–1939
American columnist and critic
Tallulah Bankhead; Critical
Abuse – plays
BROWN Pamela 1917–75
English actress
Advice
BROWN Thomas 1663–1704
English satirist
Prejudice

BROWNE Coral 1913–91
Australian actress
Costume; Quick Thinking
BRUCE Lenny 1923–66
American comedian
Motivation
BRYDEN Ronald 1927–2004
English critic
Olivier
BUCHANEN McKean 1823–72
American actor
Insults
BUCHANEN Robert 1841–1901
British playwright
Actors
BUCKINGHAM George Villiers,
2nd Duke of 1627–87
English courtier and
playwright
Critics; Playwrights;
Playwrights – Buckingham
BUNNER Henry C. 1855–96
American writer
Shakespeare
BURBAGE Richard c.1567–1619
English actor; first to
play many of the great
Shakespearean roles including
Hamlet, Lear and Othello
Actors – Burbage; Epitaphs;
Shakespeare's Plays – Othello
BURGE Stuart 1918–2002
British actor/director
Quick Thinking
BURLINGTON Michael b. 1939
English critic and writer
Peggy Ashcroft; Critical Abuse –
actors (Peter O'Toole); Olivier
BURNEY Charlotte 1761–1838

Sister of Fanny Burney
Fans
BURNEY Fanny (Madame
D'Arblay) 1752–1840
English novelist and diarist
Garrick; Shakespeare's Plays –
The Tempest; Sarah Siddons
BURNS George 1896–1996
American comedian
Actors – Carol Channing; Music
Hall
BURTON Richard (Richard
Jenkins) 1925–84
Welsh actor and film star.
Married to Elizabeth Taylor
Advice; Actors – Richard
Burton, Elizabeth Taylor;
Bad Habits; Critical Abuse –
actors; Insults; Motivation;
Shakespeare's Plays – Hamlet,
The Tempest
BYRON George Gordon, 6th
Baron 1788–1824
English poet
Acting; Sheridan; Sarah Siddons
BYRON H(enry) J(ames) 1834–84
English actor/dramatist
specializing in pantomime
Plays

CADELL Selina b. 1953
English actress
Dressing Room Talk
CAMPBELL Ken 1941–2008
British actor/writer
Shakespeare's Plays – Hamlet
CAMPBELL Mrs Patrick (née
Beatrice Stella Tanner)
1865–1940

English actress renowned for
her ready wit; close friend of
George Bernard Shaw
Actors – Basil Rathbone;
Audiences; Tallulah Bankhead;
J. M. Barrie; Costume and
Makeup; Insults; Noël Coward;
Technique; Telegrams; Touring
CAMPBELL Thomas 1774–1844
English writer; biographer of
Sarah Siddons
Actors – Master Betty
CANTOR Eddie 1892–1964
American comedian
Producers – Ziegfeld
CAPOTE Truman 1924–84
American writer
Actors
CARROLL Diahann b. 1935
American actress/singer
Dressing Room Talk
CARSON Jack 1910–63
American actor
Fans
CERVANTES Miguel de
Cervantes Saavedra 1547–1616
Spanish writer (*Don Quixote*)
Comedy
CHAMFORT Nicolas 1741–94
French writer who 'lived by
his wit'
Comedy
CHANNING Carol b. 1921
American actress
Actors – Carol Channing
CAREW Richard 1555–1620
English (Cornish) poet and
antiquary
Prompts

CHAPMAN John 1900–72
American theatre critic of the
Daily News
Critical Abuse – plays
CHEKHOV Anton 1860–1904
Russian dramatist (*The Cherry
Orchard, Uncle Vanya*)
*Finance; Life; Plays; Tennessee
Williams*
CHESTERTON G(ilbert) K(eith)
1874–1936
English novelist and critic
*Amateurs; Broadway; Oscar
Wilde*
CHETWOOD William Rufus
d. 1766 English bookseller and
dramatist
Reputation – Mrs Woffington
CHRISTIANSEN Marie
fl. 1930s/40s American actress
Slips of the Tongue
CHURCHILL Sir Winston
1874–1965 British statesman
and Prime Minister 1940–45,
1951–55
*Vivien Leigh; G. B. Shaw;
Telegrams*
CHRYSOSTOM St John *c.*347–407
Priest and writer
Opprobrium
CIBBER Colley 1671–1757 English
actor/dramatist and Poet
Laureate
*Actors – Colley Cibber; Finance;
Reputation – Anne Bracegirdle*
CLARKE Creston 1865–1910
American actor
Critical Abuse – actors
CLIVE Kitty 1711–85

English actress who worked
with Colley Cibber and Garrick
Critical Abuse – actors; Garrick
COCHRAN Sir Charles Blake
1872– 1951 English impresario
Critical Abuse – actors
COHAN George M. 1878–1942
American theatrical producer/
playwright/ songwriter
*Tallulah Bankhead; The Press;
Producers – George Cohan*
COLE John 1792–1848
British antiquary and book-
seller
*Shakespeare's Plays – Hamlet
(Kean)*
COLEMAN George 1762–1836
English dramatist
*Actors – Colley Cibber, John
Kemble*
COLERIDGE Samuel Taylor
1772–1834 English poet
*Beaumont and Fletcher; Kean;
Playwrights – Congreve*
COLLIER Jeremy 1650–1726
English churchman and moral
crusader
Opprobrium; Purpose
COMSTOCK Anthony 1844–1915
English writer
George Bernard Shaw
CONGREVE William 1670–1729
English playwright (*The Way of
the World*)
Critics; Playwrights – Congreve
CONNOLLY Cyril 1903–74
British journalist and critic
Noël Coward
COOK, William d. 1824

Irish dramatist
Dedication
COOKE Edmund Vance
1866–1932
American poet and author
Actors – Edwin Booth
COOPER Lady Diana 1892–1986
Society beauty and occasional
actress
Quick Thinking
COOPER Dame Gladys 1888–1971
English actress
Star Quality
CORNEILLE Pierre 1606–84
French tragic dramatist (*The
Cid*)
*Audiences; Playwrights –
Corneille*
CORNELL Katharine 1893–1974
American actress
*Actors – Katharine Cornell; Star
Quality*
COTTRELL Cherry 1909–96
English actress
Shakespeare's Plays – Hamlet
COWARD Sir Noël 1899–1973
English actor/playwright/
lyricist/ composer; best known
for his brittle, witty comedies
(*Private Lives, Blithe Spirit*)
*Acting; Actors – Gertrude
Lawrence; Advice; Ambition;
Auditions; Avant-garde;
Beaumont and Fletcher;
Beginnings; Charity Galas;
Chekhov; Child Actors; Noël
Coward; Critical Abuse –
actors; Critical Abuse – plays;
Criticism; Critics – Alexander*

*Woollcott; Dedication; Kitchen
Sink Drama; Method Acting;
The hunts; Plays; Playwrights
– Somerset Maugham, John
Osborne; Quick Thinking;
Recognition; Shakespeare's
Plays – Richard III (Olivier);
Technique; Telegrams; Theatre*
CRAIG Edward Gordon
1872–1966
English actor/stage designer/
writer; son of Ellen Terry
Irving; Ellen Terry
CRICHTON Kyle 1896–1960
American theatre critic
Critical Abuse – plays
CROSSE Henry *fl.* 17th century
Audiences
CUKOR George 1899–1983
Hollywood film director
*Vivien Leigh; Technique
(Charles Laughton)*
CUMBERLAND Richard
1732–1811 English dramatist
Garrick
CUSACK Sinead b. 1948
Irish actress
Acting
CUSHMAN Charlotte 1816–76
American actress, famous for
playing men's roles and in the
role of Meg Merrilees
Acting; Dedication
CUSHMAN Robert b. 1943
British theatre critic for the
Observer
*Critical Abuse – actors
(Elizabeth Taylor)*

DALY (John) Augustin 1838–99
American dramatist
Irving
DARLINGTON W. A. 1890–1979
English theatre critic for the
Daily Telegraph
Actors – Edith Evans;
Beginnings – Olivier; Critical
Abuse – plays
DAVIES Marion 1900–61
American actress; long time
companion of newspaper
magnate William Randolph
Hearst
Critical Abuse – actors
DAVIES Robertson 1913–1995
Canadian novelist/actor/
playwright
Critics
DAVIES Russell
Contemporary British
journalist
Olivier
DAVIES Thomas 1712–85
English actor/bookseller
Playwrights – Congreve
DAVIS Bette 1908–89
American actress and film star
Purpose
DAVIS Noel 1929- 2002
British actor/casting director
Audience Asides; Costume
and make-up; Greek Drama;
Technique
DELDERFIELD R.F. 1912–72
English novelist
Actors
DE MILLE Agnes 1908–93
American choreographer/

writer
Fame
DENCH Dame Judi b. 1934
British actress
Actors; Peggy Ashcroft; Success;
Technique
DENNIS Sandy 1937–92
American actress
Insults
DENT Alan 1905–78
English theatre critic
Technique
DEPARDIEU Gérard b. 1948
French actor
Actors – Gérard Depardieu
DEVINE George 1910–65
English actor/director; co-
founder of the English Stage
Company
Directors – George Devine
DICKENS Charles 1812–70
English writer (*David*
Copperfield, Bleak House)
Actors – Charles Dickens;
Advice
DIETZ Howard 1898–1983
American lyricist and librettist
Tallulah Bankhead; Failure
DILLER Phyllis 1917–2012
American comedienne
Actors – Phyllis Diller
DODD Ken(neth Arthur)
1931–2018 British comedian
Comedy; Life
DORAN Dr John 1807–78
English social historian
Playwrights – Aphra Behn
DOVER Kenneth James
1920–2010 English scholar;

professor of Greek
Greek Drama

DREW John 1853–1927
American actor, uncle of Ethel,
John and Lionel Barrymore
Actors – John Drew

DRUMMOND William 1585–1649
Scottish poet
Playwrights – Ben Jonson

DRYDEN John 1631–1700
English poet
*Actors – Nell Gwynne;
Beaumont and Fletcher; Life;
Playwrights – Buckingham;
Shakespeare; Shakespeare's
Plays – The Tempest*

DUDLEY William b. 1947
English theatre designer
Critics – Kenneth Tynan

DUMAS Alexandre 1824–95
French novelist/playwright
Sarah Bernhardt; Prejudice

DU MAURIER Sir Gerald 1873–
1934 English actor-manager
Actors – Gerald Du Maurier

DUNCAN Ronald 1914–82
British playwright
Playwrights

D'URFEY Thomas 1653–1723
British dramatist and song-
writer
Opprobrium

DURANTE Jimmy (James
Francis) 1893–1980
American actor/comedian,
known as 'Schnozzle'
Shakespeare's Plays – Hamlet

DUSE Eleonora 1859–1924
Italian actress

*Actors – Eleonora Duse; Critical
Abuse – actors; Theatre*

ELDON John, 1st Earl of 1751–1838
English lawyer and politician
Sheridan

ELLIOTT Denholm 1922–92
English actor
Costume and Make-up

ELIOT T(homas) S(teams)
1883–1965 American-born
poet/critic/dramatist (*Murder
in the Cathedral*)
*Beaumont and Fletcher; Critical
Abuse – plays; Critics – Hazlitt;
Musicals; Plays; Purpose*

ELLISTON Robert W. 1774–1831
English actor
*Actors – Robert Elliston; Critical
Abuse – actors*

ERVINE St John 1883–1971
English playwright and theatre
critic
Audiences

ESSLIN Martin 1918–2002
Hungarian born critic and
writer
Avant-garde; Directors

EURIPIDES 480–406 BC
Greek tragedian
Playwrights – Euripides

EVANS Dame Edith 1888–1976
English actress remembered
for her definitive portrayal of
Lady Bracknell in Wilde's *The
Importance of Being Earnest*
*Actors – Edith Evans;
Shakespeare's Plays – Macbeth;
Technique; Touring*

EVANS Gareth Lloyd
Contemporary British theatre
critic
Playwrights – Harold Pinter
EVELYN John 1620–1706
English diarist
Shakespeare's Plays – Hamlet

FADIMAN Clifton 1904–99
American writer
Playwrights – Clare Boothe Luce
FALLON Gabriel b. 1923
Irish writer
Mrs Patrick Campbell
FELDMAN Marty 1933–83 British
actor and comedy writer
Comedy
FERBER Edna 1887–1968
American writer; member of
the Algonquin Round Table
*Critics – A. Woollcott; Producers
– Jed Harris*
FERGUSON Elsie 1885–1961
American actress
Telegrams
FERNALD John 1905–85
American-born theatre
director
Audience Asides
FEYDEAU George 1862–1921
French dramatist, author of
more than 60 farces
Playwrights – Feydeau
FFRANGCON-DAVIES Dame
Gwen 1891–1991 British actress,
famous for her Juliet, with
John Gielgud, in 1924; played
her last television part aged 100
Advice; Auditions; Ellen Terry

FIELD Eugene 1850–95
Theatre critic of the *Denver
Tribune* in the 1880s
Critical Abuse – actors
FIELDING Henry 1707–54
English novelist (*Tom Jones*)
*Actors; Critical Abuse – plays;
Shakespeare's Plays – Hamlet*
FIELDS W(illiam) C(laude)
Dukinfield 1880–1946
American vaudeville comedian
and film star
*Actors; Actors – Mae West;
Advice*
FINDLATER Richard 1921–85
British theatre critic
*Peggy Ashcroft; Critical Abuse –
plays; Theatre*
FINNEY Albert b. 1936
British actor
*Finance; Shakespeare's Plays –
Hamlet*
FISHER Eddie 1928–2010
American singer
Insults
FISKE Minnie Maddern (Marie
Augusta Davey) 1865–1932
American actress
*Actors – Minnie Maddern Fiske;
Technique*
FITZGERALD Barry 1888–1961
Irish actor
Actors – Barry Fitzgerald
FLECKNOE Richard d. 1678 Jesuit
priest and playwright
Epitaphs
FLETCHER John 1579–1625
English dramatist, collaborator
with Beaumont

Beaumont and Fletcher

FO Dario 1926–2016
Italian playwright/actor
Playwrights; Tragedy

FOGARTY Elsie 1866–1945
Founder of the Central School
of Speech Training and
Dramatic Art, London
Technique

FONTAINE Joan 1917–2013
American actress
Vivien Leigh

FONTANNE Lynn 1887–1983
American actress, wife of
Alfred Lunt
Insults; The Lunts

FOOTE Samuel 1720–77
English actor/dramatist
Critical Abuse – actors; Epitaphs

FORBES-ROBERTSON Sir
Johnstone 1853–1937
English actor-manager
Dedication

FORD John (Sean O'Feeney)
1895– 1973
American film director *Acting;
Actors – Barry Fitzgerald*

FOWLER Gene 1890–1960
American writer
Barrymores (John)

FREDERICK (Antoine-Louis-
Prosper Lemaitre) 1800–76
French actor of Romantic
drama
Actors – Frederick

GABRIEL Gilbert W. 1890–1952
American theatre critic of *The
World*, 1930s

Critical Abuse – plays

GAINSBOROUGH Thomas
1727–88 English landscape and
portrait painter
Sarah Siddons

GARLAND Judy (Frances
Gumm) 1922–69
American actress/singer/
dancer
Insults; Stage Fright

GARLAND Robert 1895–1955
American theatre critic
Chekhov; Critical Abuse – plays

GARRICK David 1717–79
English actor-manager;
renowned for his versatility
and the naturalism of his
acting
*Comedy; Epitaphs; Fame; Fans;
Garrick; Prologues; Scenery and
Lighting; Sheridan; Technique;
Telegrams*

GAXTON William 1893–1963
American actor
Telegrams

GENET Jean 1909–86
French playwright/novelist/
poet; credited with creating the
'Theatre of Cruelty'
Technique

GEORGE II 1683–1760
King of Great Britain and
Ireland 1727–60
Shakespeare

GEORGE III 1738–1820
King of Great Britain and
Ireland 1760– 1820
Shakespeare

GEORGE VI 1895–1952

King of Great Britain and
Northern Ireland 1936–52
Ralph Richardson
GERHARDIE William 1895–1977
English writer
*Playwrights – Somerset
Maugham*
GIBBS (Oliver) Wolcott 1902–58
American theatre critic for the
New Yorker
*Critical Abuse – plays; The
Theatre*
GIELGUD Sir John 1904–2000
British actor/director
*Actors – Vanessa Redgrave; Film
and Television; John Gielgud;
Shakespeare's Plays – Hamlet;
Technique*
GILBERT Sir William Schwenck
1836–1911 English poet/
dramatist; librettist of the
Gilbert and Sullivan comic
operas (*The Mikado, The
Pirates of Penzance*); built and
owned the Garrick Theatre
*Dressing Room Talk; Epitaphs;
Insults; Irving; Shakespeare's
Plays – Hamlet; Success;
H. B. Tree*
GILDER Rosamund 1896–1986
American writer and dramatic
critic
Theatre
GILDON Charles 1665–1724
English critic and playwright
Actors – Mary Betterton
GILL Brendan 1914–97
American writer
Tallulah Bankhead

GILLIATT Penelope 1933–93
English writer; theatre critic of
the *Observer* 1964–68
*Peggy Ashcroft; Playwrights –
Beckett*
GINGOLD Hermione 1897–1987
English comedy actress
*Actors – Donald Wolfit;
Beginnings; Billing*
GIRAUDOUX Jean 1882–1944
French playwright
Plays
GISH, Lillian 1893–1993
American actress
Insults
GLENVILLE Peter 1913–96
English director
Film and Television
GOGARTY Oliver St. John
1878– 1957
Irish poet and memoir writer
Playwrights – Lady Gregory
GOLDSMITH Oliver 1728–74
Irish playwright (*She Stoops to
Conquer*), and novelist
Garrick; Epitaphs
GOODWIN Nat(haniel) Carl
1857–1919 American comedian
Broadway
GONCOURT Edmond de
1822–96 French novelist;
founder of the Academie
Goncourt
Sarah Bernhardt
GORDON Ruth 1896–1985
American actress; married to
writer Garson Kanin
Acting; Critical Abuse – actors
GRAVES Robert 1895–1985

English poet and novelist
Shakespeare
GREENE Sir Graham 1904–91
British novelist
Success
GREENE Robert 1558–91
English dramatist
Shakespeare
GREGORY Lady 1852–1932
Irish playwright associated
with the Abbey
Theatre
Playwrights – Lady Gregory
GREVILLE Samuel *fl.* 1767
First recorded American
professional actor
Beginnings
GRIFFITH Hubert 1896–1953
British drama critic and
dramatist
Critical Abuse – actors; Olivier
GUEDALLA Philip 1889–1944
English historian and
biographer
J. M. Barrie
GUINNESS Mrs *fl.* 1890s
Member of Frank Benson's
Shakespeare Company
Quick Thinking
GUINNESS Sir Alec 1914–2000
English actor
*Critics – Kenneth Tynan; John
Gielgud*
GUTHRIE Sir (William) Tyrone
1900–71
English actor and director
*Advice; Directors; Film and
Television; Olivier; Talent*
GWYNNE Nell (Eleanor)

*c.*1650–87 English actress,
mistress of Charles II
Actors – Nell Gwynne

HAGGARD Stephen 1911–43
English actor, co-author with
Athene Seyler of *The Art of
Comedy*
Comedy
HALE Lionel 1909–76 British
journalist and playwright
Critical Abuse – plays
HALL George b. 1925
Former Director of the Acting
Course at the Central School of
Speech and Drama in London
Dressing Room Talk
HALL Sir Peter 1930–2017
British director/producer.
Created the Royal Shakespeare
Company 1960; succeeded
Olivier as Director of the
National Theatre
*Peggy Ashcroft; Audiences;
Costume and Make-up; Critics;
Directors; Directors – Peter
Hall; Finance; First Nights; Life;
Plays; Playwrights – Brecht; The
Press; Rehearsals; Restoration
Theatre; Shakespeare;
Shakespeare's Plays – Hamlet;
Success; Theatre*
HAMMOND Percy 1873–1936
American theatre critic for the
New York Herald Tribune
Critical Abuse – plays; Criticism
HAMPTON Christopher b. 1946
British playwright (*Les Liaisons
Dangereuses*)

Critics

HANDS Terry b. 1941 British
theatre director. Associated
most closely with the Royal
Shakespeare Company
Motivation

HAPGOOD Norman 1868–1937
American theatre critic
Shakespeare's Plays – Hamlet

HARDWICKE Sir Cedric
1893–1964 British actor
*Actors; Actors – Cedric
Hardwicke; Critical Abuse –
actors; Film and Television;
Technique*

HARE Augustus 1792–1834
English clergyman and writer;
brother of Julius Hare
Life

HARE David b. 1947
British playwright (*Plenty,
Pravda*)
Purpose

HARE Julius 1795–1855
English clergyman and
essayist; brother of Augustus
Hare
Life

HARRIMAN Margaret Case
c.1904– 1966
American journalist whose
father (Frank Case) had run
the Algonquin Hotel during
the heyday of the Algonquin
Round Table
Tallulah Bankhead

HARRIS Frank 1856–1931
British writer and journalist
Shakespeare; G. B. Shaw

HARRIS Jed 1900–79
American theatrical producer
*Critics; Epitaphs; Producers –
Jed Harris*

HARRIS Richard 1930–2002
Irish actor
*Actors – Richard Harris;
Shakespeare's Plays – Cymbeline*

HARRISON Sir Rex 1908–90
British actor and film star
Beginnings

HART Moss 1904–61 American
playwright and director
Plays

HAUSER Frank 1922–2007
British theatre director
Motivation

HAYES Helen (Brown) 1900–93
American actress, the 'First
Lady' of American theatre
*Actors – Helen Hayes; Critical
Abuse – actors; Fame; Purpose;
Theatre*

HAZLITT William 1778–1830
English essayist and theatre
critic for *The Examiner* and
The Morning Chronicle
*Critics – Hazlitt; Finance;
Kean; Shakespeare; Sheridan;
Sarah Siddons*

HECHT Ben 1894–1964
American journalist
Sarah Bernhardt

HEINE Heinrich 1797–1856
German poet and essayist
Playwrights – Schiller

HELLMAN Lillian 1905–84
American playwright (*The
Little Foxes*)

Tallulah Bankhead; Playwrights
– Lillian Hellman
HELPMANN Robert 1909–86
Australian-born actor/dancer/
choreographer
Musicals
HEMINGWAY Ernest 1899–1961
American war correspondent
and novelist (*For Whom the
Bell Tolls*)
Failure; Insults
HEPBURN Katharine 1907–2003
American actress and film star
Acting; Critical Abuse – actors
HERFORD Oliver 1863–1935
American writer
Actors
HEROLD Don 1889–1966
American journalist
Noël Coward
HESTON Charlton 1922–2008
American actor and film star
Actors – Richard Harris
HICKS Sir (Edward) Seymour
1871–1948
English actor-manager
Amateurs
HILL Benny 1925–92
British comedian
Show Business
HILLER Dame Wendy b. 1912
British actress
Method Acting
HELLGATE Jason
Contemporary British
journalist
Shakespeare's Plays – Hamlet
HOBSON Sir Harold 1904–92
English theatre critic for the

Sunday Times for over 40 years
*Shakespeare's Plays – Hamlet,
Othello*
HOFFMAN Dustin b. 1937
American actor and film star
Advice
HOFFMAN Irving fl. 1930s/40s
New York correspondent for
the *Hollywood Reporter*
Critical Abuse- plays
HOPE Anthony (Sir Anthony
Hope Hawkins) 1863–1933
English novelist (*The Prisoner
of Zenda*)
*J. M. Barrie; Epitaphs – W. S.
Gilbert*
HOPE Bob 1903–2003 American
comedian and actor
Audiences
HOPPER Hedda 1890–1966
American actress turned gossip
columnist
Actors – Hedda Hopper
HORDERN Sir Michael 1911–95
British actor
Critical Abuse – actors
HOUDAR DE LA MOTTE
Antoine 1672–1731
French poet/playwright
Censorship
HOUSSAYE Arsene fl. 1899
Director of the Comédie
Française
Playwrights
HOWARD Leslie 1893–1943
English actor and film star
Shakespeare's Plays – Hamlet
HUGO Victor 1802–85
French poet/novelist (*Les

Misérables), and playwright
(*Ruy Blas*)
Playwrights – Victor Hugo
HUNEKER James 1860–1921
American theatre critic for *The
Sun* and *The New York Times*
Ibsen
HUNT Hugh 1911–93
English writer and director
Insults
HUNT (James Henry) Leigh
1784–1859
English poet and essayist
*Actors – Robert Elliston, J. P.
Kemble; Critics*
HURREN Kenneth 1920–93
British theatre critic
Critical Abuse – actors
HUXLEY Aldous 1894–1963
British novelist (*Brave New
World*)
Greek Drama
HYDE WHITE Wilfrid 1903–90
British actor
*Beginnings; Critical Abuse –
actors; Directors; Oscar Wilde*

IBSEN Henrik 1828–1906
Norwegian poet and dramatist
(*A Doll's House, Ghosts*)
*Mrs Patrick Campbell; Critical
Abuse – plays; Ibsen*
IONESCO Eugene 1912–94
Romanian-born French
playwright
Playwrights – Ionesco; Theatre
INVERCLYDE Lady June 1901–85
English actress
Insults

IRVING Sir Henry 1838–1905
English actor-manager. First
actor to be knighted for
services to the theatre. Enjoyed
a phenomenal success with *The
Bells.* Ran the Lyceum Theatre
with Ellen Terry as his leading
lady
*Advice; Fame; Scenery and
Lighting; Shakespeare's Plays –
Richard III; Ellen Terry*

JACKSON Glenda b. 1936 British
actress and politician
*Beginnings; Directors – Peter
Hall; Technique*
JACOBI Derek b. 1938
British actor
Acting; Advice; Stage Fright
JAMES Clive b. 1939
Australian-born writer and
critic
Olivier
JAMES Henry 1843–1916
Anglophile American novelist
Acting; Irving; Ellen Terry
JARVIS Martin b. 1941
British actor
Film and Television
JEANS Ronald 1887–1973
English actor
Actors; First Nights
JEFFERSON Joseph 1829–1905
American actor/comedian
Technique
JENNINGS H. J. *fl.* c.1910
English journalist
Critical Abuse – plays
JEROME Jerome K(lapka) 1859–

1927 English playwright and
writer (*Three Men in a Boat*)
*Beginnings; Critical Abuse –
plays; Finance*
JESSEL George 1898–1981
American actor/producer
Quick Thinking
JOHNSON Celia 1908–82
British actress best
remembered for her role
in the film *Brief Encounter*
Actors – Celia Johnson
JOHNSON Richard 1927–2015
British actor and film star
Film and Television
JOHNSON Dr. Samuel 1709–84
English lexicographer/critic
*Actors; Actors – Thomas
Sheridan; Criticism; Epitaphs –
Goldsmith, Garrick; Playwrights
– Corneille; Prologues;
Shakespeare; Sarah Siddons*
JONES Henry Arthur 1851–1929
Prolific and successful English
playwright (*The Silver King*)
*Insults; Playwrights – Henry
Jones; G. B. Shaw*
JONSON Ben 1572–1637
English poet and dramatist
(*Volpone*); contemporary of
Shakespeare who appeared
in his play *Every Man in His
Humour*
*Actors – Alleyn, Burbage;
Beaumont and Fletcher;
Epitaphs; Shakespeare; Theatre*
JOUVET Louis 1887–1951
French director/actor
Avant-garde

JOYCE James 1882–1941
Irish writer (*Ulysses*)
G. B. Shaw

KAEL Pauline 1919–2001
American film and theatre
critic
Insults
KALEM T. E. 1920–85
American journalist
Tennessee Williams
KAUFMAN George S.
1889–1961 American playwright
(*The Man Who Came to
Dinner*) and wit
*Critical Abuse – actors; Critical
Abuse -plays; Epitaphs;
Producers -Jed Harris;
Telegrams*
KAUFMAN Wolfe 1905–70
American journalist
Vivien Leigh
KEAN Edmund 1789–1833
The most famous English
actor of his day. Renowned
for playing the major
Shakespearean roles at Drury
Lane.
*Comedy; Kean; Shakespeare's
Plays – Hamlet, Romeo and
Juliet*
KEATING Fred 1897–1961
American actor
Tallulah Bankhead
KEMBLE Charles 1775–1854
English actor specializing in
romantic parts such as Romeo;
brother of John Kemble and
Sarah Siddons, father of Fanny

Kemble
Slips of the Tongue
KEMBLE Fanny (Francis) 1809–
93 English actress and writer,
niece of Sarah Siddons
Kean
KEMBLE John Philip 1757–1823
English tragedian; brother of
Sarah Siddons
Actors – J. P. Kemble; Kean
KENDAL Dame Margaret
(Madge) 1845–1939
English actress
Sarah Bernhardt; Child Actors;
Quick Thinking
KENNEDY Joseph P. 1888–1969
American self-made multi-
millionaire and sometime
Ambassador to the United
Kingdom
Actors
KERR Deborah 1921–2007
British actress best
remembered for her role in the
film *The King and I*
Actors – Deborah Kerr
KERR Jean 1923–2003
American playwright, wife of
Walter Kerr
Actors; Adaptations; Audiences;
Comedy
KERR Walter F. 1913–96
American journalist and critic;
husband of Jean Kerr
Actors – Elizabeth Taylor;
Critical Abuse – plays; Critics;
Producers – David Merrick
KITCHIN Laurence 1913–97
English writer

Actors
KLEIN John David
Contemporary American
theatre critic
Critical Abuse – plays
KNOWLES Sheridan 1784–1862
Irish dramatist
Sarah Siddons
KRETZMER Herbert b. 1925
British journalist and theatre
critic
Critical Abuse – plays
KRONENBURGER Louis
1904–80
American theatre critic
Critical Abuse – plays (Mae
West)

LACTANTIUS Lucius Caelius *fl.*
4th century AD
Christian theologian
Comedy
LAMB Charles 1775–1834
English essayist; author, with
his sister Mary, of *Tales of*
Shakespeare
Finance; Shakespeare's Plays –
Hamlet
LANDOR Walter Savage
1775–1864 English poet
Shakespeare
LANGFORD Bonnie b. 1964
English singer/dancer/actress;
former child star
Child Actors; Critical Abuse –
plays
LANGNER Lawrence 1890–1962
American co-founder of the
Theater Guild

born in Maine, USA of English
parents
G. B. Shaw

LICHTENBERG Georg Christoph
1742–99
German physicist and satirist
Shakespeare

LILLIE Bea(trice) (Lady Peel)
1898–1989
Canadian born comedienne
*Actors – Bea Lillie; Insults
(Tallulah Bankhead)*

LINCOLN Abraham 1809–65
16th President of the United
States. Assassinated during a
visit to the theatre
Comedy; Shakespeare

LIPMAN Maureen b. 1946
British actress/writer
Shakespeare; Quick Thinking

LISTER Moira 1923–2007
English actress
Critical Abuse – actors

LITTLEWOOD (Maudie) Joan
1914–2002 English director,
founder of Theatre Workshop
Actors; Producers

LIVINGS Henry 1929–98
English actor
Costume and Make-up

LLOYD Marie (Matilda Alice
Victoria Wood) 1870–1922
British music hall star, famous
for her risqué songs
Epitaphs; Music hall/Vaudeville

LOGAN Joshua 1908–88
American playwright/producer
Chekhov

LONGFORD Lady (Christine

Patti Trew) 1900–80
Irish playwright
Critical Abuse – plays

LOVE Montague 1897–1943
English actor
Critical Abuse – actors

LUCE Clare Boothe 1903–87
American playwright
Playwrights – Luce

LUNT Alfred 1893–1977
Highly successful American
actor/ producer/director.
Married to Lynne Fontanne
The Lunts

McCAMBRIDGE Mercedes
1916–2004 American actress
Critics – A. Woollcott

McCAREY Leo *fl.* 1950s
American journalist
Star Quality

MacCARTHY Sir Desmond
1877–1952 English critic
G. B. Tree

MACAULAY Thomas Babington,
1st Baron 1800–59
English historian and essayist
*Actors – Anne Bracegirdle;
Playwrights – Wycherley*

McEWAN Geraldine 1932–2015
English actress
Critical Abuse – actors

MACLIAMMOIR Micheal
(Alfred Willmore) 1899–1978
Irish actor. Co-founder of the
Gate Theatre in Dublin
Acting; Star Quality

McCOWEN Alec 1925–2017
British actor

Beginnings; Vivien Leigh;
Technique

McKELLEN Sir Ian b. 1939
British actor
Shakespeare's Plays – Hamlet

MACREADY William Charles
1793– 1873
English actor, rival of Kean
Actors – Master Betty; Irving;
Technique

McSHANE Ian b. 1942
British actor
Film and Television

MAETERLINCK Count Maurice
1862–1949
Nobel Prize winning Belgian
playwright. Renowned for his
erudition and involvement in
the symbolist movement
Mrs Patrick Campbell; Critical
Abuse – plays; Playwrights –
Maeterlinck

MAMET David b. 1947
American playwright
(*Glengarry Glen Ross*)
Playwrights – Mamet

MANEY Richard 1891–1968
American theatre publicist
Dressing Room Talk

MANKIEWICZ Herman J. 1897–
1953 American playwright;
co-wrote *Citizen Kane* with
Orson Welles
Playwrights – Orson Welles

MARCH Frederic 1897–1975
American actor
Critical Abuse – actors

MARLOWE Christopher 1564–93
English dramatist

(*Tamburlaine the Great,*
The Tragical History of Dr.
Faustus)
Beaumont and Fletcher;
Playwrights – Marlowe

MARTIN Mary 1913–90
American actress best known
for her role in the musical
South Pacific
Broadway; Recognition; Talent

MARX Harpo (Arthur) 1893–1964
American actor/comedian; one
of the Marx Brothers
Critical Abuse – plays; Oscar
Levant

MARX Groucho (Julius)
1890–1977
American actor/comedian; one
of the Marx Brothers
Critical Abuse – plays

MARX Karl 1818–63
German founder of
international communism
Shakespeare's Plays – The Merry
Wives of Windsor

MASON BROWN John 1900–69
American journalist; theatre
critic of *The Saturday Review of*
Literature
Adaptations; Critics – A.
Woollcott; Olivier; Playwrights
– O'Neill; Shakespeare's Plays –
Antony and Cleopatra (Tallulah
Bankhead)

MASSEY Daniel 1933–98
British actor; son of Raymond
Massey and godson of Noël
Coward
Actors – Gertrude Lawrence;

Noël Coward; Star Quality

MASSEY Raymond 1896–1984
Canadian-born actor/director
Critical Abuse – actors

MASSON Tom 1866–1934
American actor/critic
Shakespeare's Plays – Hamlet

MATTHAU Walter 1920–2000
American actor
*Acting; Film and Television;
Vivien Leigh*

MATTHEWS A(lfred) E(dward)
1869–1960
English actor
Critical Abuse – actors

MATURA Mustapha b. 1939
West Indian-born playwright
Playwrights – Mustapha Matura

MAUGHAM (William) Somerset
1874–1965
British novelist and playwright
(*The Circle*)
*Plays; Playwrights – Somerset
Maugham*

MENCKEN H(enry) L(ouis)
1880–1956
American writer and critic
Comedy; Finance; Shakespeare

MEREDITH Burgess 1907–97
American actor/director/
producer
Telegrams

MEREDITH George 1828–1909
English novelist (*Diana of the
Crossways*)
Comedy

MERMAN Ethel 1904–84
American actress/singer
Talent (Mary Martin)

MERRICK David 1911–2000
American producer/actor
*Critics; Producers – David
Merrick*

MILES Sir Bernard 1907–91
English actor/manager;
founder of the Mermaid
Theatre
Purpose

MILLER Arthur 1915–2005
American playwright (*The
Crucible*)
Playwrights – Arthur Miller

MILLS Sir John 1908–2005
English actor
*Audience Asides; Costume and
Make-up*

MILNE A(lan) A(lexander)
1882–1956 English novelist/
playwright (*Mr Pym Passes By*)
and children's writer (*Winnie
the Pooh*)
*Actors – Du Maurier;
Audiences; Plays; Playwrights*

MILTON Ernest 1890–1974
British actor
Advice

MILTON John 1608–74
English poet (*Paradise Lost*)
Shakespeare

MITFORD Mary Russell
1787–1855 English novelist and
dramatist
Kean

MIZNER Addison 1872–1933
American architect
Actors

MIZNER Wilson 1876–1933
American actor/playwright/

entrepreneur and Broadway
character
Actors; Finance
MOLIÈRE (Jean Baptiste
Poquelin) 1622–73
French playwright (*Le
Misanthrope, Le Malade
Imaginaire*)
Playwrights – Molière
MOLNÁR Ferenc (Neumann)
1878–1952
Hungarian novelist and
playwright (*The Good Fairy*)
Success
MOORE George 1852–1933
Irish novelist (*Esther Waters*);
helped found the Abbey
Theatre in Dublin
*Acting; Motivation; Theatre;
Oscar Wilde*
MORAND Paul 1889–1975
French diplomat and writer
Broadway
MORE Hannah 1745–1833
English writer
Shakespeare's Plays – Hamlet
MOREHOUSE Ward 1899–1966
American writer
Ziegfeld
MORLEY Robert 1908–92
English actor
Actors; Advice; Playwrights
MORLEY Sheridan 1941–2007
English writer and critic, son of
Robert Morley
*Critical Abuse – plays;
Playwrights – Beckett*
MORSE Robert b. 1931
American actor

Theatre
MORTIMER John 1923–2009
British lawyer/novelist/
playwright (*A Voyage Round
My Father*)
Plays
MOSS Hugh *fl.* 1910
English actor
H. B. Tree
MUNI Paul (Muni
Weisenfreund) 1895–1967
American-Yiddish actor *Advice*
MURPHY Tom b. 1935
Irish playwright
Playwrights – Tom Murphy

NADZO Guido *fl.* 1930s
American actor
Critical Abuse – actors
NASH (Frederic) Ogden 1902–71
American poet who wrote
light/comic verse
Noël Coward
NATHAN George Jean 1882–1958
American writer and theatre
critic for *Vanity Fair* and
Newsweek
*Actors; Actors – Eleonora Duse;
Tallulah Bankhead; J. M.
Barrie; Noël Coward; Critical
Abuse – plays; Critics – G. J.
Nathan; First Nights; Musicals;
Music hall; Plays;
Playwrights – Sartre;
Shakespeare's Plays – Hamlet*
NIETZSCHE Friedrich 1844–1900
German philosopher and critic
Playwrights – Hugo
NIGHTINGALE Benedict

b. 1939 British theatre critic
Directors – Peter Brook;
Playwrights – Mustapha Matura
NIVEN David (James Nevins)
1910–83
English actor and film star
Acting; Barrymores (John)
NOBLE Adrian b. 1950
British theatre director;
Artistic Director of the Royal
Shakespeare Company
Theatre
NORTHBROOKE John *fl.* 1570
English preacher and moralist
Opprobrium
NOVELLO Ivor (David Ivor
Davies) 1893–1951 Welsh actor/
playwright and composer
(*Keep the Home Fires Burning*)
Actors – Novello; Critical Abuse
– plays; Recognition
NUGENT Frank 1908–65
American critic
Critical Abuse – actors

ODETS Clifford 1906–63
American left-wing playwright
Critical Abuse – plays
OLIVER Freddie b. 1962
British writer
Oscar Wilde
OLIVIER Sir Laurence Kerr
(Baron Olivier) 1907–89
English actor/director/
producer renowned for
the physical energy of his
acting. Widely regarded
as the foremost English
speaking actor of the 20th

century. Played all the great
Shakespearean roles, most
notably Richard III, Hamlet,
Othello and Henry V. Married
to Vivien Leigh 1940– 61.
Director of the National
Theatre 1962–73
Acting; Actors – Deborah Kerr,
Anthony Quayle, Donald
Wolfit; Advice; Audience Asides;
Beginnings; Costume and Make-
up; Fame; Life; Motivation; The
Press; Purpose; Shakespeare's
Plays – Hamlet, Henry V,
Merchant of Venice, Othello,
Romeo and Juliet; Star Quality;
Success; Talent; Technique
O'NEILL Eugene 1888–1953
American playwright (*The*
Iceman Cometh)
Playwrights – O'Neill
ORIGEN AD 185–254
Early Christian church father
and school master
Censorship
OSBORNE John 1929- 94
English playwright (*Look Back*
in Anger). Pioneer of realism in
post-war theatre
Noël Coward; Criticism;
Critics; Directors – George
Devine; Musicals; Music hall;
Plays; Playwrights; Playwrights
– J. Osborne; Rehearsals;
Shakespeare's Plays – Hamlet;
G. B. Shaw; Stage Management;
Touring
O'TOOLE Fintan b. 1958
Irish critic and writer

Playwrights – Tom Murphy
O'TOOLE Peter 1932–2013
  Irish actor and film star
  (*Lawrence of Arabia*)
  Bad Habits; Actors – O'Toole;
  Critical Abuse – actors
OVID (Publius Ovidius Naso) 43
  BC – AD 17 Latin poet
  Audiences

PAAR, Jack 1918–2004 American
  comedian
  Oscar Levant
PACK Major Richardson
  1682–1728 English soldier and
  writer
  Playwrights – Wycherley
PAGNOL Marcel 1895–1974
  French playwright
  Broadway
PALMER Lilli (Peiser) 1914–86
  German-born actress working
  in UK and America
  G. B. Shaw
PARKER Dorothy 1893–1967
  American writer/humorist/
  critic; member of the
  influential Algonquin Round
  Table group of critics
  Actors – Edith Evans; Critical
  Abuse – actors (Marion Davies);
  Critical Abuse – plays; Critics –
  Dorothy Parker; Epitaphs; First
  Nights; Oscar Wilde
PATRICK David 1849–1914
  English writer and editor
  (*Chambers Encyclopaedia of*
  English Literature)
  Actors – Colley Cibber

PEARSON Hesketh 1887–1964
  British actor and biographer
  G. B. Tree
PEMBERTON Brock 1886–1950
  American writer
  Critics –A. Woollcott
PEPYS Samuel 1633–1703
  English diarist
  Actors – Nell Gtvynne;
  Shakespeare's plays – Macbeth,
  Midsummer Night's Dream,
  Romeo and Juliet
PETAN Zarco 1929–2014
  Slovenian theatre director
  Directors
PINERO Sir Arthur Wing
  1855–1934 English playwright
  (*The Gay Lord Quex*)
  Kean; Playwrights – Pinero
PINTER Harold (Harold Da
  Pinta) 1930–2008
  British playwright (*The*
  Birthday Party, No Man's Land)
  Critical Abuse – plays;
  Playwrights – Pinter
PIRANDELLO Luigi 1867–1936
  Italian dramatist (*Six*
  Charactersin Search of an
  Author)
  Playwrights – Pirandello
PLATO *c.* 427–*fl.* 347 BC
  Athenian philosopher, disciple
  of Socrates
  Playwrights – Aristophanes
PLOWRIGHT Joan b. 1929
  English actress. Third wife of
  Laurence Olivier
  Olivier
PLUMMER Christopher b. 1929

Canadian actor based in
Hollywood
Actors -Julie Andrews
POLLOCK Channing 1880–1946
American playwright and critic
Critics
POPE Alexander 1688–1744
English poet and satirist
Audiences; Garrick; Shakespeare
PORTER Cole 1891–1964
American composer and
lyricist
Motivation; Shakespeare
PORTMAN Eric 1903–69
British actor
Star Quality; Technique
POTTER John S. 1806–69
American actor-manager
Finance
PRIESTLEY J(ohn) B(oynton)
1894– 1984 English novelist and
playwright (*Dangerous Comer,
When We Are Married*)
Actors
PRITCHARD Hannah 1711–68
English actress
Dedication
PRYNNE William 1600–69
English Puritan pamphleteer
Opprobrium

QUAYLE Sir (John) Anthony
1913–89 British actor/director/
manager; director of the
theatre at Stratford-upon-Avon
1948–56
Actors – Anthony Quayle
QUAYLE Douglas 1904–57 British
actor

Advice; Epitaphs
QUAYLE John b. 1938
British actor
Advice
QUILLEY Denis 1927–2003
British actor
Critical Abuse – actors
QUIN James 1693–1766 English
tragedian of the declamatory
school of acting
Auditions
QUINN Anthony 1915–2001
American actor
Technique

RACHEL (Elisa Felix) 1821–58
French tragedienne, famous for
her interpretation of Racine's
Phedre
Actors; – Rachel; Insults
RATHBONE Basil 1892–1967
South African-born actor,
famous in the role of Sherlock
Holmes
Actors – Basil Rathbone
RATTIGAN Sir Terence 1911–79
English playwright (*French
Without Tears, The Winslow
Boy*)
Audiences
REDGRAVE Sir Michael 1908–85
English actor
Olivier
REDGRAVE Vanessa b. 1937
British actress, daughter of
Michael Redgrave and Rachel
Kempson. Holds radical
political views
Actors – Vanessa Redgrave;

Advice; Theatre

REED Rex b. 1938
American theatre critic
Tennessee Williams

REYNOLDS Sir Joshua 1723–92
English portrait painter
Garrick

RICH Frank b. 1949
American theatre critic
sometimes known as the
Butcher of Broadway
Musicals; Producers – David Merrick

RICHARDS Dick *fl.* 1950s/60s
English show business
journalist and theatre critic
Noël Coward; Kean

RICHARDSON Sir Ralph 1902–83
English actor
Acting; Actors – Sybil Thorndike; Advice; Audiences; Criticism; Film and Television; Ralph Richardson; Shakespeare's plays – Hamlet, Othello; Technique

RICHARDSON Tony 1928–92
English theatre and film
director (*Tom Jones*)
Theatre

RIGG Diana b. 1938
British actress
Insults

ROBINSON David b. 1930
British journalist and film
critic
Actors – Gérard Depardieu

ROBINSON Edward G. (Emanuel
Goldenberg) 1893–1973
American actor and film star

Barrymores (Ethel)

ROBINSON Henry Crabb
1775–1867 English diarist
Critical Abuse – actors; Sarah Siddons

ROBINSON Jay 1930–2013
American actor/producer
Critical Abuse – actors

ROGERS Ginger (Virginia)
1911–95 American actress/film
star/dancer, famous for her
screen partnership with Fred
Astaire
Advice

ROGERS Samuel 1763–1855
English poet and essayist
Garrick; Scenery and Lighting

ROSE Billy 1899–1966
American impresario and
circus proprietor known as The
Midget Maestro of Broadway
Tallulah Bankhead; Critical Abuse – plays; Finance; Oscar Levant; Producers – Billy Rose

RUGGLES Eleanor 1916–2008
American biographer
Dedication

RUNYON (Alfred) Damon
1884–1946
American journalist and short
story writer. The musical *Guys and Doth* was based on one of
his stories
Broadway

RUSSELL Bertrand, 3rd Earl
1872–1970
English philosopher/
mathematician/pacifist
G. B. Shaw

RUTHERFORD Dame Margaret
1892–1972
British actress
Actors – Margaret Rutherford
RYMER Thomas 1641–1731
English critic
Shakespeare's plays – Othello

SAINTSBURY George 1845–1933
English writer and scholar
Playwrights – Molière
SAKI Pen-name of H(ector)
H(ugh) Munro 1870–1916
British novelist and short story
writer
G. B. Shaw
SALINGER J(erome) D(avid)
1919–2010 American novelist
(*Catcher in the Rye*)
Opprobrium
SANDERS George 1906–72
British actor and film star
Acting; Actors
SARTRE Jean Paul 1905–80
French existentialist
philosopher/political activist/
literary critic, novelist and
playwright (*Huis Clos, Kean*)
Actors; Motivation
SCHILDKRAUT Joseph
1895–1964
Austrian-Yiddish actor
working in the USA
Insults
SCHULER (Johann) Friedrich
1759–1805
German dramatist and poet
Playwrights – Schiller
SCOFIELD Paul 1922–2008

British actor
Critical Abuse – actors
SCOTT Clement 1841–1904
English theatre critic for the
*Daily Telegraph, Sporting and
Dramatic News*
Actors; Ibsen
SCOTT Sir Walter 1771–1832
Scottish novelist (*Ivanhoe*) and
poet
Audiences
SEVERO Richard b. 1932
American writer
Actors – Monty Woolley
SEYLER Athene 1889–1990
British actress; author, with
Stephen Haggard, of *The Craft
of Comedy*
*Actors – Athene Seyler; Comedy;
Costume and Make-up*
SHAKESPEARE William
1564–1616
English dramatist and poet,
born in Stratford-upon-Avon.
Generally accepted as the
world's greatest playwright.
The most performed dramatist
in the world, his 37 plays
include *Midsummer Night's
Dream, Romeo and Juliet,
Twelfth Night, Hamlet, Othello*
and *King Lear.*
*Actors – Colley Cibber;
Advice; Critical Abuse – plays;
Epilogues; Epitaphs; Life;
Plays; Playwrights – Corneille;
Shakespeare; Shakespeare's
Plays; G. B. Shaw; Star
Quality*

SHARIF Omar 1932–2015
Egyptian-born actor and film star
Actors – Peter O'Toole

SHAW George Bernard 1856–1950
Irish critic/playwright (*St. Joan, Pygmalion*) with radical beliefs about everything from vegetarianism to capitalism
Acting; Actors; Actors – Eleonora Duse, Cedric Hardwicke; Ambition; Audiences; J. M. Barrie; Beaumont and Fletcher; Mrs Patrick Campbell; Censorship; Costume and Make-up; Critical Abuse – plays; Criticism; Critics; Directors; Epitaphs; Finance; Insults; Irving; Vivien Leigh; Plays; Playwrights; Playwrights – Maeterlinck, Marlowe; Shakespeare; G. B. Shaw; R. B. Sheridan; Telegrams; Ellen Terry; Oscar Wilde

SHERIDAN Richard Brinsley 1751–1816
Irish politician and playwright (*The School for Scandal, The Rivals*)
Critics; Plays; Purpose; R.B. Sheridan

SHERIDAN Thomas 1719–88
Irish actor; father of R.B. Sheridan
Actors – Thomas Sheridan

SHERWOOD Robert 1896–1955
American playwright (*Abe Lincoln in Illinois, Tovarich*)

The Lunts

SHOALES Ian b. 1949
American critic
Musicals

SHULMAN Milton 1913–2004
Canadian-born British theatre critic for the *Evening Standard*
Critical Abuse – actors

SIDDONS Mrs (nee Sarah Kemble) 1755–1831
English actress. The foremost tragedienne of her generation
Sarah Siddons; Technique

SIDDONS William 1744–1818
English actor, husband of Sarah Siddons
Sarah Siddons

SIGNORET Simone 1921–85
French actress
Actors – Hedda Hopper; Shakespeare's plays – Macbeth

SIMON John b. 1925
American theatre critic
Critical Abuse – actors; Insults

SINDEN Donald 1923–2014
English actor
Advice

SKINNER Otis 1858–1942
American actor
Barrymores (Maurice)

SKINNER Cornelia Otis 1902–79
American actress and diseuse
Telegrams

SMITH Dame Maggie (Natalie) b. 1934 British actress
Beginnings

SOTHERN Edward Askew (Douglas Stewart) 1826–81
English actor who worked

successfully for long periods in
the United States
Quick Thinking

SPATE Roger
Contemporary British
journalist
Critical Abuse – actors

STANISLAVSKI Constantin
(Sergeivitch Alexeyev)
1865–1938 Russian actor/
producer/teacher; developed
a scheme for teaching acting
technique based on the
psychology of the characters
portrayed and the actor's
innate capacity for self-
expression. This was later
developed by Lee Strasberg as
'Method' acting
*Advice; Insults; Method Acting;
Technique*

STEPHENS Yorke 1862–1937
English actor
Critical Abuse – actors

STERN G. B. 1890–1973
American journalist
The Lunts

STEVENS Ashton 1872–1951
American writer
Actors – Bea Lillie

STEYN Mark
Contemporary British
journalist
Musicals

STEYNE Geoffrey *fl.* 1917
American actor
Critical Abuse – actors

STIRLING Fanny 1813–95
English actress famous for her

comedy roles
Actors

STOPPARD Tom b. 1937
Czechoslovakian-born British
playwright (*Rosencrantz
and Guildenstern are Dead,
Jumpers*)
*Critical Abuse – plays; Plays;
Playwrights – Tom Stoppard*

STOREY David 1933–2017
English playwright (*Home, The
Changing Room*)
Critical Abuse – plays

STRACHEY (Giles) Lytton
1880–1932 English biographer
Oscar Wilde

STRASBERG Lee 1901–82
American director/producer/
teacher; founder of the Actors'
Studio in New York where
he worked with actors using
the methods developed by
Stanislavski
Method Acting

STRINDBERG August 1849–1912
Swedish playwright (*Miss Julie,
The Dance of Death*)
Playwrights – Strindberg

STUBBES Philip d. 1593
English Puritan pamphleteer
Opprobrium

SWAFFER Hannan 1879–1962
American critic
Critical Abuse – plays

SWINBURNE Algernon C.
1837–1909
English poet and critic
*Playwrights – Marlowe; Oscar
Wilde*

SYDNEY Sir Philip 1554–86
English poet
Scenery and Lighting

TASHMAN Lilyan 1900–34
American actress
Ambition
TALMADGE Norma 1897–1957
American actress
Fans
TAYLOR Elizabeth 1932–2011
British-born American actress
and film star (*National Velvet,
Cat on a Hot Tin Roof*)
*Actors – Richard Burton,
Elizabeth Taylor*
TEMPEST Dame Marie (Mary
Susan Etherington) 1864–1942
English actress
Actors – Marie Tempest
TENNYSON Alfred, Lord
1809–1902 English poet
Playwrights – Ben Jonson
TERRY Dame Ellen 1847–1928
English actress; her
partnership with Henry Irving
at the Lyceum dominated
London theatre in the late 19th
century
*Advice; Beginnings (Olivier);
Irving; Shakespeare's Plays
– Macbeth; G. B. Shaw; Star
Quality; Technique*
THOMAS Dylan 1914–53
Welsh poet (*Under Milk Wood*)
G. B. Shaw
THORNDIKE Dame Sybil
1882–1976
British actress who played the

title role in the first production
of Shaw's *St. Joan*
*Actors; Actors – Sybil
Thorndike; Ellen Terry*
TOLSTOY Count Leo
Nikolayevich 1828–1910
Russian novelist (*War and
Peace*) and philosopher
*Censorship; Chekhov; Critical
Abuse – plays; Shakespeare*
TREE, Sir Herbert Beerbohm
1853– 1917 English actor-
manager, half brother of
Max Beerbohm; Tree was a
flamboyant character actor and
keen rival of Henry Irving
*Advice; Bad Habits; Clubs;
Directors; Fame; Playwrights;
Shakespeare's Plays – Hamlet;
G. B. Tree*
TREE Lady Helen (Maud)
1863–1937 English actress most
successful in comic roles.
Married to Herbert Beerbohm
Tree
Technique
TREWIN J(ohn) C(ourtenay)
1908–90 British theatre critic
for the *Observer*
Failure; Vivien Leigh
TRINDER Tommy 1909–89
British comedian
Pantomime
TROLLOPE Frances 1780–1863
English novelist/travel writer;
mother of Anthony Trollope
Shakespeare
TROUGHTON Patrick 1920–87
British actor

Critical Abuse – plays
WARNER Jack 1892–1978
Hollywood producer, founder
of Warner Brothers
Barrymores (John)
WARRISS Ben 1909–93
British comedian, one half
of the partnership Jewell and
Warriss
Comedy
WAUGH Evelyn 1903–66
English novelist (*Brideshead
Revisited, Scoop*)
Oscar Wilde
WEIR George *fl.* 1920s
English actor
Bad Habits
WELLES (George) Orson 1915–85
American actor/writer/
director. Best known for his
films *Citizen Kane* and *The
Third Man*
*Actors; Failure; Playwrights
– Orson Welles; The Press;
Shakespeare*
WELLS H(erbert) G(eorge)
1866–1946 English novelist and
sociologist (*War of the Worlds*)
Shakespeare; G. B. Shaw
WERTENBAKER Timberlake
b. 1929
American-born playwright
Theatre
WESKER Arnold 1932–2016
British playwright (*Chips With
Everything*)
Kitchen Sink
WEST Mae 1892–1980
American actress/producer/

writer (*Diamond Lit, She Done
Him Wrong, Catherine Was
Great);* famous for one-liners
redolent with sexual innuendo
*Actors – Mae West; Audiences;
Critical Abuse – plays; Epilogues*
WHISTLER James Abbot McNeill
1834–1903 American painter
who worked mainly in England
Oscar Wilde
WHITE E. B. 1899–1985
American writer
Critics
WHITE Thomas 1550–1624
English Puritan writer
Opprobrium
WHITELAW Billie 1932–2014
British actress who worked
closely with Samuel Beckett
Dedication
WHITING John 1917–63
British playwright (*Marching
Song, The Devils*)
Actors
WILDE Oscar Fingal O'Flahertie
Wills 1854–1900
Irish playwright (*Lady
Windermere's Fan, The
Importance of Being Earnest*)
and wit; his aphorisms are
frequently quoted
*Acting; Actors; Advice;
Audiences; Critical Abuse –
plays; Criticism; Critics – M.
Beerbohm; Epitaphs; Irving;
Plays; Playwrights; The Press;
Shakespeare's Plays – Hamlet,
Macbeth; G. B. Shaw; Success;
Ellen Terry; H. B. Tree*